CLAIRE MACKAY

TOUCHING ALL THE BASES

BASEBALL FOR KIDS OF ALL AGES

FIREFLY BOOKS

A Boardwalk Book

ILLUSTRATED BY BILL SLAVIN

W9-AVX-708

A FIREFLY BOOK

Published in the U.S. in 1996 by:
Firefly Books (U.S.) Inc.
P.O. Box 1338
Ellicott Station
Buffalo, New York 14207

Original text by Claire Mackay and original illustrations by Bill Slavin, copyright © 1994. Published by arrangement with Scholastic Canada Ltd. and Boardwalk Books.

Cataloguing in Publication

Mackay, Claire, 1930
    Touching all the bases

Includes index.

ISBN 1-55209-000-0

1. Baseball-Juvenile literature. I. Slavin, Bill. II. Title.

GV867.5.M24 1996   j796.357   C95-932460-7

Produced by Boardwalk Books for Firefly Books (U.S.) Inc.

Edited by Charis Wahl
Design, Electronic Composition and Production by Blair Kerrigan/Glyphics

Credits

Text: **10:** excerpt from "Analysis of Baseball" by May Swenson used with the kind permission of R.R. Knudson, Executor of the Estate **67:** words to "Take Me Out to the Ball Game" reproduced by permission of the Jerry Vogel Music Company, Inc. **76:** original scorecard reproduced from *Baseball By The Rules* (c) Glen Waggoner, Kathleen Moloney, and Hugh Howard **87:** "The New Kid" used with the kind permission of Mike Makley

Pictures: Front Cover: The Stock Market **Back Cover:** photo of Claire Mackay by Peter Carver **Page 5:** (top right) illustration from *A Little Pretty Pocket-Book*, originally published by John Newbery in 1744, taken from a facsimile edition in The Osborne Collection of Early Children's Books, Toronto Public Library **7:** National Baseball Library & Archive, Cooperstown, N.Y. **9:** (bottom) Negro Leagues Baseball Museum (top right) National Baseball Library & Archive, Cooperstown, N.Y. **11:** (bottom right) from *Bat, Ball, Glove: The Making of Major League Baseball Gear* by William Jaspersohn. Copyright (c) 1989 by William Jaspersohn. By permission of Little, Brown and Company **19:** Behac/Canada Wide used with the permission of the Minnesota Twins Baseball Club **20:** The Stock Market **23:** National Baseball Library & Archive and The Bettmann Archive **26:** (left) The New York Yankees' photograph of Yankee Stadium was reproduced with the permission of the New York Yankees (bottom) the Astrodome was reproduced with the permission of Astrodome USA **27:** (top) Mark O'Neill/ Canada Wide (bottom) Oriole Park at Camden Yards used with the kind permission of Ron Richards **34:** National Baseball Library & Archive **38/39:** (middle) National Baseball Library & Archive **41:** (left) Claus Andersen/Masterfile (right) National Baseball Library & Archive used with the kind permission of Pam Postema **43:** (c) Sobel-Klonsky/The Image Bank Canada **47:** all photos from the National Baseball Library & Archive **49:** National Baseball Library & Archive **52:** (top) National Baseball Library & Archive (middle) Canapress Photo Service (Hans Deryk) used with the kind permission of the Toronto Blue Jays Baseball Club (bottom) Behac/Canada Wide, used with the kind permission of the Minnesota Twins Baseball Club **53:** National Baseball Library & Archive and Canapress Photo Service **54:** (middle) National Baseball Library & Archive (bottom) Canapress Photo Service (Bill Grimshaw) used with the kind permission of Buck Martinez (right) Gary Carter used with the kind permission of the Montreal Expos **55:** (top) Negro Leagues Baseball Museum (bottom) National Baseball Library & Archive **57:** National Baseball Library & Archive **59:** all photos from the National Baseball Library & Archive **60:** Canapress Photo Service (Phill Snel) used with the kind permission of the Cleveland Indians **68:** photo supplied by *The Sporting News* **69:** photo of Sherry Davis used with the kind permission of the San Francisco Giants **70:** National Baseball Library & Archive **71:** National Baseball Library & Archive **81:** Canapress Photo Service and World Wide Photo **88:** National Baseball Library & Archive **Note:** The American League, National League, and Club trademarks depicted herein were reproduced with permission from Major League Baseball Properties, Inc.

All rights reserved. No part of this publication may be reproduced or stored in a retrieval system, or transmitted in any form or by any means, electronic, mechanical, recording, or otherwise, without the written permission of the publisher, or under a licence from the Canadian Reprography Collective.

Color Separations by Compeer Typographic Services Limited
Printed and Bound in Canada by Tri-graphic Printing (Ottawa) Limited

To Nicky and Dan Scrimger, life-long fans, life-long friends
— CM

For my nephews — Josh, Jake, and Kyle
— WS

Acknowledgments

Touching All the Bases might never have reached first without a great lineup of people who helped. My thanks to the staff at the Osborne Collection of Early Children's Books, who never strike out; novelist Alison Gordon, sportswriter James Davidson, and Peter Widdrington, Chairman, Toronto Blue Jays Baseball Club, keen-eyed readers who told me when I'd dropped the ball; John and Chieko Wales, fluent fans of Japanese baseball; Rich Morris of Hollywood Bases, Inc., a fast man with a fax; Tyler Kepner, whose baseball card appears on page 69; and Marian Hebb, who led me away from foul territory. I owe a special thanks to the heart of the order: Nicky and Dan Scrimger, to whom the book is dedicated, for talk, tickets, and telephone calls; Bernice Bacchus, world champion mother and researcher; my husband Jack, steadfast pinchrunner of errands, household appliances, and life in general; and my editor Charis Wahl, who coached me through the whole nine innings, blocked most of my wild pitches, and notched another save.

— Claire Mackay

CONTENTS

1ST INNING

THE GAME & HOW IT GREW

"It's about youth and dreams and fame and success and failure and inspiration and devotion."
Writer unknown

Let's get one thing straight: baseball did not begin with Abner Doubleday on a field in Cooperstown one summer day in 1839. It's a beloved bit of folklore, but it's not true.

Abner Doubleday was a soldier who did brave deeds at Gettysburg during the American Civil War. He also wrote in his diary every day of his adult life, and not once did he mention baseball. Besides, he was nowhere near Cooperstown in 1839. Doubleday probably watched baseball, and maybe even played it, but he did not invent it.

The whole story was made up in 1907 by Alfred G. Spalding, former star pitcher of the Boston Red Stockings, club owner, and millionaire maker of sporting goods. Al dug up a fellow named Abner Graves, who swore he'd seen the other Abner create the game. He even claimed the word "baseball" had been coined by Doubleday. Spalding, you see, just couldn't stand the thought that baseball might not really be American.

The truth is this: Bat-and-ball games were played by children (and grown-ups) for centuries before Doubleday was born. The ancient Egyptians and the not-quite-so-ancient Aztecs played a game much like baseball. (For all we know, the first cave children played baseball as soon as they found a round rock and a long stick.)

The dictionary tells us that the word "base-ball" was first written in 1700 by Reverend Thomas Wilson of Maidstone, Kent, England, when he gave the village kids a hard time for playing the game on Sundays. (In London, the same game was called "feeder," and in western England, "rounders.") And in 1744 the word appeared in one of the first books for children, *A Little Pretty Pocket-Book*, published by John Newbery, who is known as the father of children's books — even though he made most of his money from a phony medicine called Dr. James's Fever Powder. In the *Pocket-Book* are verses describing popular games and sports for children. One of those verses is entitled "Base-Ball," and its first four lines are:

> *The Ball once struck off,*
> *Away flies the Boy*
> *To the next-destin'd Post,*
> *And then Home with Joy.*

A woodcut illustration shows a "feeder" (pitcher) about to make an underhand throw, and two "posts" (bases) with a boy standing by each of them. (The bat, flat and wide at the end, was often called a "club"; and the catcher was called a "scorcher.")

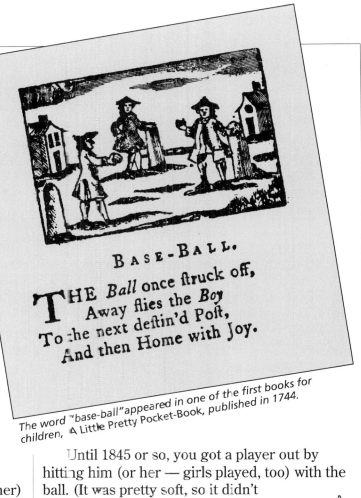

BASE-BALL.

THE *Ball* once ftruck off,
Away flies the *Boy*
To the next deftin'd Poft,
And then Home with Joy.

The word "base-ball" appeared in one of the first books for children, A Little Pretty Pocket-Book, published in 1744.

Until 1845 or so, you got a player out by hitting him (or her — girls played, too) with the ball. (It was pretty soft, so it didn't hurt much but your pride.) Then New York Knickerbocker pitcher Alexander Cartwright (whose day job was counting money at a bank) came up with the idea of the tag: the runner would be out if touched with the ball held by a fielder. (That wasn't his only idea Cartwright, together with Dr. Daniel Adams — the first man to play shortstop — wrote down the basic rules of the game.) This simple change meant that teams could now use a hard ball, which could be hit much farther; baseball was now a game for grown men.

Throughout the 19th century, North America was studded with diamonds: every village had its ballpark, every city and town its grandstand, every hamlet its nine. Each school and college, factory and mill, police station and hardware store, church and saloon had a team. From April to October, it seemed as if the whole continent did little but hit, run, and throw.

Then someone came up with a shocking idea: if baseball's so popular, why don't the best players get paid? Make it their job? The rich gentlemen who played for fun were horrified. Their game might be taken over by "rascals and riff-raff." Newspapers warned that the hired "mercenaries" would turn baseball into "a game for gamblers." Clergymen prophesied a nation sunk in sin.

In fact, teams had been secretly paying players for years. Some played for the highest bidder and jumped from team to team. (They were promptly dubbed "revolvers.") In Canada's flourishing baseball clubs, paid American players were called "the Foreign Legion."

The first team on which all players played ball for a living was the Cincinnati Red Stockings, started in 1869. They were an instant success: their record quickly climbed to 137 wins and four losses. The teams who lost all those games learned fast: they scoured the country for the best players — and paid them. Professional baseball had arrived. And the newspapers and clergymen were right: bribes and gambling were soon part of the game. Baseball had problems. Baseball needed rules.

To solve the problems and to set the rules, eight powerful owners — with clubs in Philadelphia, Hartford, Boston, Chicago, Cincinnati, Louisville, St. Louis, and New York — formed the National League in 1876. Within weeks the League banned gambling, liquor, Sunday games, and contract-jumping. Dishonest players were expelled for life. Then the League got a little power-mad. It told the players they couldn't leave the teams that hired them — even though those very same teams could fire them for any reason at all. Then it told the players they had to provide their own uniforms, buy their own meals — and take a big cut in pay. The players were not happy.

Club owners in other cities weren't happy, either. They saw the crowds flowing into League parks and the cash flowing into League pockets — and they wanted a piece of the action. So, in 1901, they formed the American League and two years of baseball war began. Bitter battles were fought over territory, ticket sales, player contracts, trades, and transfers. Then, in 1903, the National League surrendered. There would be two leagues, each with eight clubs. And so it stayed for half a century.

Aside from one huge scandal (see box), baseball was calm, baseball was peaceful, baseball was popular — and baseball was tidy. Baseball the *game* still is. But in the last 40 years, baseball the *business* has been very messy.

THE CHICAGO BLACK SOX SCANDAL

Players were not paid much in the early years, and the temptation to make a little money on the side was sometimes too hard to resist. In 1919, a few players didn't resist — and baseball was very nearly ruined. The Chicago White Sox, one of the greatest teams in history, met the Cincinnati Reds in the best-of-nine World Series. The Sox were a sure bet to win — until pitcher Eddie Cicotte made a deal with local gamblers. The fix was in. The Reds won the Series, five games to three.

Rumors swirled, accusations flew, and the next year a grand jury investigated. Cicotte spilled the beans and named the players who from that day to this are known as the Black Sox: Eddie Cicotte, pitcher Lefty Williams, Buck Weaver, Swede Risberg, Chick Gandil, Happy Felsch, Fred McMullin, and batting hero Shoeless Joe Jackson — whose shocked fans begged him to "say it ain't so, Joe." And it might not have been so, for Joe: he hit over .300 in the Series.

Presiding over the jury was grim-jawed, white-haired Kenesaw Mountain Landis, a stern and upright judge who once fined John D. Rockefeller $29 million, and later suspended Babe Ruth for barnstorming. The players were acquitted the following year — after their confessions mysteriously disappeared — but Landis, by that time baseball's first commissioner, banned them from baseball for life.

Shoeless Joe, a magnificent hitter with a .356 career average, was exiled, perhaps unjustly, from his field of dreams. In one of baseball's odd twists of fate, a man who copied Jackson's "pretty swing" would help to heal the hurt of the Black Sox scandal and bring new glory to the game. His name was Babe Ruth.

COMMISSIONER LANDIS: A MOUNTAIN OF A MAN?

On June 27, 1864, Union Army surgeon Abraham Landis got a nasty leg wound at the Battle of Kennesaw Mountain in Georgia. He vowed that if he kept his leg he'd name his first son after the place where the wound healed. His leg got better, his son was born — and the poor kid had to answer to Kenesaw Mountain (spelled wrong) the rest of his life. Lucky his dad didn't get shot at Popocatepetl.

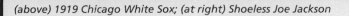

(above) 1919 Chicago White Sox; (at right) Shoeless Joe Jackson

EXPANSION FEVER

Expansion fever hit in the 1960s, and it hasn't stopped yet. There are still two leagues, but each league has three divisions: East and Central with five teams apiece, and West with four. That makes 28 teams — and by the time you read this book, there may be more. Two of those teams — the Montreal Expos and the Toronto Blue Jays — aren't even in the United States, and Al Spalding may be spinning in his patriotic grave.

The players had their own notion of expansion. They got a good union and expanded their power off the field. They won the right to have a say in where they play and what they earn — which is sometimes enough to buy a small country or two.

But even players' salaries are small potatoes compared to what teams get from television. Not that long ago, CBS paid $1,000,000,000 for the right to televise major league games for four years. Clubs in big cities such as New York, Chicago, and Toronto, where more people watch the games — and the commercials — get more dollars from television than clubs in smaller cities such as Seattle and Cleveland. This means the big clubs get richer and can afford better players, while the poor teams get poorer and some disappear altogether.

It can't last. Something's got to give. Big changes are coming, and once again baseball has nasty problems. But it will endure, as it has since Alexander Cartwright and his friends first wrote down the rules, as it has since John Newbery first wrote his poem about it, as it has since children first played a game with a bat and a ball.

BLACKS

On a Sunday back in 1797, the town constable of Fayetteville, North Carolina, was ordered to give 15 lashes "to Negroes seen playing baseball." This attitude stuck for 150 years: if you were black, baseball could be dangerous to your health. About 35 black players made it to the major league level during the 1880s, but none of them stayed long. A few white players welcomed them, but most didn't: some walked off the field; others sharpened their spikes or pitched at the heads of black batters.

The baseball field was too often a battlefield. White fans — who sat well away from black fans — weren't all that pleasant either. They entertained themselves with vicious name-calling, insults, and threats of lynching. By 1890, the only blacks on major league fields were mascots or clowns. Despite the Civil War, Emancipation, and Abraham Lincoln — who was playing baseball when he heard he'd been nominated for President — big-league ball had no room for black players.

So they made a room of their own. Many black teams made their living barnstorming, that is, playing — and usually winning — anywhere, any time, against anybody. They also amused the fans: the All-American Black Tourists sported top hats, full tuxedos, and silk umbrellas. The Page Fence Giants rode into town on bicycles. But behind the fun was tremendous talent. Catcher Josh Gibson, credited with 800 homers, once hit a ball so high and so far that nobody saw it again. Shortstop John Henry "Pop" Lloyd, whom a white sportswriter called the best player in baseball history, had a batting average of .564 when he was 44 years old. And Smokey Joe

IN BASEBALL

Williams, whose fastball was a hot blur, pitched a 12-inning game and struck out 27 batters.

The first professional black team, the Cuban Giants of Long Island, was formed in 1885. Soon there were many more teams, enough to organize the Negro National League in 1920, and three more Leagues before 1930. For a while the Negro Leagues attracted fans and made money, but they struggled during the Great Depression and World War Two. And not long after Jackie Robinson ran onto Ebbets Field with his eight white teammates, the Negro Leagues disappeared.

Who was the first black player in major league baseball? If you answered Jackie Robinson, you're wrong. On the first day of May, 1884, 63 years before Robinson put on a Brooklyn Dodgers uniform, Moses Fleetwood Walker (pictured above) crouched behind home plate in Toledo, Ohio. The son of a doctor and a star athlete in college, Fleet Walker was snapped up by Toledo, then a team in the American Association, an early major league. With no mask, no glove, no chest protector, Fleet played hurt much of the time; but even with a broken rib he batted .263. But his time in the "bigs" was short: in a few years all black players were barred from major league baseball.

1945 Kansas City Monarchs

9

2ND INNING

THE GEAR

It's about
the ball,
the bat,
and the mitt.
Ball hits bat,
or it hits mitt.

"Analysis of Baseball,"
May Swenson (1971)

THE BALL

In the beginning was the ball. No ball, no ball game. Did anyone ever sing, "Take me out to the bat game?" Did anyone ever buy a ticket to sit in the base park? No, of course not. No ball, no ball game.

In earlier, simpler bat-and-ball games such as rounders, trap ball, and one-old-cat, the ball was soft and hollow. Just as well, too: you got strikers (runners) out by throwing the ball at them. If the ball struck a body, the owner of the body was out. With a harder ball, your ancestor might not have lived to be one.

The same soft ball was used in the first years of baseball — until Cartwright's "tagged-out" rule in 1845, where the runner is out if touched by the ball *held* by an opposing player. Not thrown — held. That meant they could now use a serious ball, a hard ball.

But how big? How heavy? Made of what? Nobody could decide. One early model, with a core of melted rubber, measured 8½ inches (21.5 cm) around — about the size of your average apple — and weighed only three ounces (85 grams). The scoreboard often read "Home 127, Visitors 83." A larger and heavier ball (11 inches around and 6 ounces; 28 cm and 170 grams) didn't help: no pop, not much bounce. Only a thud. It was like playing with a bag of beans.

Finally, in 1872, the rulemakers made up their minds: an official baseball must weigh 5 to 5$\frac{1}{4}$ ounces (141 to 148 grams) and be 9 to 9$\frac{1}{4}$ inches (22.8 to 23.5 cm) in circumference.

And so it remains. The ball thrown by 22-year-old ace pitcher Albert Goodwill Spalding (yes, he who made up the Doubleday story and made millions making official major-league baseballs) of the 1872 Boston Red Stockings was the same size and weight as that thrown 30 years later by mean-tempered Denton True "Cy" (for "Cyclone") Young (yes, he whose name is on the Best Pitcher of the Year Award) of the Boston Pilgrims, and, 90 years after that, by Roger Clemens (yes, "The Rocket," three-time winner of the Cy Young Award) of the Boston Red Sox.

Same size, same weight — but what's *inside* the ball has changed. The years from 1880 to 1910 or so saw the era of the "dead ball," made of very little rubber but lots of wool. Games played with a dead ball were full of bunts, hit-and-run plays, and stolen bases. Home runs were rare — the Chicago White Sox, who won the American League pennant in 1906, hit just six all season. One early ball player said, "The only way you could hit a homer was if the outfielder tripped and fell down."

In 1910 George Reach invented the cork-centered ball, with a layer of rubber around the cork: the dead ball sprang to life, and Al Spalding's factory swung into production. The "live ball," or "rabbit ball," era had arrived, and home runs doubled in two years.

Nowadays Rawlings (who took over from Spalding in 1973) makes all major league baseballs. The materials are manufactured in the United States, but the last step, the sewing, is done in Costa Rica. Here's the recipe: Coat a cork sphere with 2 layers of rubber. Wind it with 121 yards (111 m) of blue-gray wool yarn, 45 yards (41 m) of white wool yarn, 53 yards (48.5 m) of blue-gray wool yarn, and 150 yards (137 m) of fine cotton yarn. Coat with rubber cement. Wrap in a two-piece cowhide cover. Hand-stitch with 108 red cotton stitches.

cotton stitches

cork nucleus

rubber

cowhide cover

wool yarn

cotton yarn

A baseball is hand-stitched with exactly 108 stitches.

As in any great recipe, there is a secret ingredient. It is mud. Not just any mud, but Lena Blackburne's Baseball Rubbing Mud. Lena (real name Russell) was a not-very-good manager (99 wins, 133 losses with the Chicago White Sox in 1928 and 1929), but a great salesman. He found some excellent mud near his New Jersey home and persuaded the bosses of baseball to buy it from him. Ever since, men sworn to secrecy row to a special place somewhere along the Delaware River, and, in the dark of night, gather mud. It is sifted, put into cans, and shipped out to every team in the major leagues. Before a game the umpires rub about 12 dozen baseballs with Lena's mud. The shiny white ball turns a light tan color, which reduces the glare, and the grain of the cowhide is raised, which makes for a better grip. When you figure that each of the 28 major league teams uses about 18,000 balls per season, Lena Blackburne's Baseball Rubbing Mud, at $75 per can, is neither dirt cheap nor cheap dirt.

Inaugural Balls

On opening day in 1993, all three members of the United States' First Family threw baseballs: President Bill Clinton threw the first pitch in Baltimore, Hillary Clinton in Chicago's Wrigley Field for her beloved Cubs, and 13-year-old Chelsea in Ohio for the Triple A Dayton Cubs.

The $200,000 baseball?

On September 30, 1927, 14-year-old Herb Siegel sat in the right-field bleachers at Yankee Stadium. He worshipped Babe Ruth, who in 1921 had hit a record 59 home runs. With only two games left in the season, Ruth had equaled his record. Would he — could he — break it?

That afternoon, in his last at-bat of the game, the Babe smashed an inside curveball over the right-field fence, 10 feet (3 m) from the foul pole and about five feet (1.5 m) from Herb. Dozens scrambled for it, but Herb Siegel grabbed it from under the seats. Ruth offered the boy five dollars and another baseball, but Herb smiled and said no.

When he died Herb left the ball to his son George. Fifteen years later, in an auction on May 2, 1992, the top bid for the famous Babe Ruth Ball was $200,000.

Only thing is that the October 1, 1927, issue of *The New York Times* reported that the famous ball was caught by 40-year-old Joe Forner of Manhattan. So what's the real story?

THE BAT

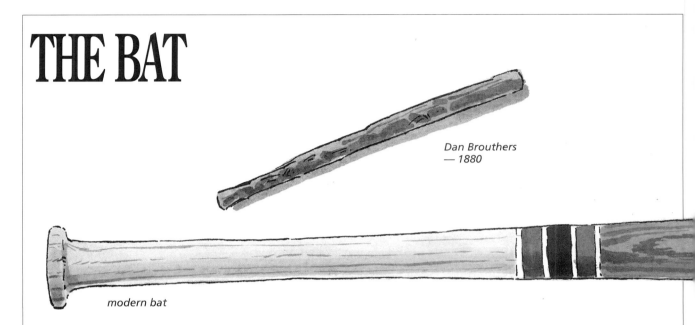

Dan Brouthers — 1880

modern bat

In the beginning, the bat wasn't a bat. A pioneer Canadian player, remembering games played in Ontario in the 1830s, said: "The club (we had bats in cricket, but we never used bats in baseball) was generally made of the best cedar, blocked out with an axe and . . . finished with a . . . knife. A wagon spoke, or any nice straight stick would do."

Cedar is light and easily shaped. It smells good, makes great shingles and canoes, and it's full of Vitamin C. (It cured explorer Jacques Cartier's sailors of scurvy back in 1535. They boiled the leaves and bark and drank the resulting "tea," then smeared the dregs on their swollen joints.) But it's also soft, and it splinters if you hit it hard. When the ball got harder, players switched to hickory, a strong, tough, heavy wood, much in demand for barrel hoops, ax handles, and fuel — with the nuts being used for pecan pie. In his first seasons Babe Ruth sometimes used a hickory bat weighing 56 ounces (1.6 kg). There's no weight limit for a bat: you can swing a 10-pound log if you can lift it off your shoulder. But the length — 42 inches (107 cm) — hasn't changed since 1868, and the width, at the thickest part, was set at 2¾ inches (7 cm) in 1895.

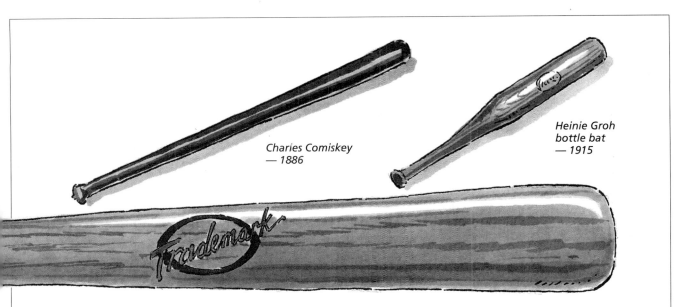

Charles Comiskey
— 1886

Heinie Groh
bottle bat
— 1915

For many players hickory was too heavy, and the tree of choice became white ash, which grew in the northeastern United States, Nova Scotia, and southern Quebec. Ash is hard, durable, and light: perfect for skis, oars, snowshoes, tennis racquets — and baseball bats. Back in the days of knights, ash was perfect for lances. An ash lance was easy to lift, easy to handle even at 16 feet long (5 m), and strong enough to impale an enemy. What was good for the Round Table was fine for the diamond. Things go better with ash — including baseballs.

The best-known batmaker is Hillerich & Bradsby, which manufactures the "Louisville Slugger." It all started in 1884, when Pete Browning, an outfielder with the Louisville Eclipse, asked an 18-year-old woodworker named John "Bud" Hillerich to make him a bat. Bud did, and the following season Pete's average soared to .362. (This made up for his terrible fielding. Nicknamed "The Gladiator," Pete fought with hundreds of fly balls — and lost.) The word got out, and the orders came in.

They're still coming in: now located near Louisville, in Jeffersonville, Indiana, H & B makes 3,000,000 Sluggers a year.

Other folks make bats, too. The Worth Company makes the "Tennessee Thumper." Rawlings has a huge factory in New York's Adirondack Mountains. (Good name: "adirondack" means "tree-eater.") There they make bats for such stars as Darryl Strawberry and Dave Winfield. Cooper bats are made in Hespeler, a little town near Guelph, Ontario — whose Maple Leaf baseball team beat the Boston Red Stockings in 1872. Cooper bats are now in the hands of Cecil Fielder, Mark McGwire, Jose Canseco, and Robbie Alomar.

Players do weird and wonderful things with their bats. Frankie Frisch, an infielder for the Giants and Cardinals in the 1920s and 1930s, hung his bats in a barn like a row of sausages. Ty Cobb, a Detroit outfielder (1905-28) who never hit below .300, rubbed his bat with a cow's thigh-bone, while second baseman Eddie Collins buried his bats in a manure pile, "to keep them alive." With a lifetime average of .333, Eddie came up smelling like roses.

WANT TO MAKE A BAT?

First, find an ash tree about 50 years old. Cut it down. Lug it to the factory.

Take the bark off. Saw and split and shape it until you have a pile of 40-inch (102 cm) long, 3-inch (7.6 cm) round cylinders, called "billets."

Dry the billets in an oven as big as a building for a month or so. Or dry them without an oven, the way H & B does — but it will take a couple of years.

Put the billets, one by one, into a "copy lathe" — a cutting and shaping machine that makes each bat an exact copy of the model a player uses, which you have on file in your bat "library." (It's like getting a duplicate of your front-door key at a hardware store.)

Then you sandpaper the bat, pass it through a flame to harden the wood, and, if the player asks, coat it with lacquer or paint, either black or brown — no other colors are allowed.

Your last job is stamping the bat with the company trademark. Unless a batter wants it somewhere else, the trademark goes where the grain is widest, which is where the wood is weakest. Players are taught from Little League on to "keep the trademark up," facing the sky. Why? To hit the ball harder, and to avoid broken bats.

2 or 2,000?

The average professional player uses 72 bats in a year. Babe Ruth used 170 one year — he gave many away — but Hall of Famer Lou Gehrig used only half a dozen a season. Bill Terry, of the New York Giants, needed only two bats to reach an average of .401 and win the 1930 batting crown. Then there is first baseman Orlando Cepeda, who believed that each bat had only one hit in it. After he got a hit, he threw the bat away. His career hit total was 2,351.

Illegal Weapons — Hollow Promises, Top Secrets, and Cover-Ups

It's against the rules to tamper with regulation bats, but batters still try now and then. A favorite trick is corking: you remove the end of a bat, hollow out the barrel, fill it with cork (or styrofoam or, in one case, mercury) and glue the end back on. The cork makes the bat lighter. The lighter the bat, the faster the swing — one ounce (28 grams) lighter = one mile (1.6 km) per hour faster. A hollow bat would be perfect, but it would break if you hit the ball. Astro Billy Hatcher was caught cork-handed in 1987. His bat hit the ball, shattered, and sprayed bottle-cap liners all over home plate and the umpire. He was tossed out of the game.

The most famous outlaw bat belonged to three-time hitting champ George Brett of the Kansas City Royals. George loaded up the bat handle with pine tar — a sticky liquid that gives the batter a good grip. In a game against the Yankees, on July 24, 1983, Brett stepped into the batter's box.

It was the top of the ninth, with two out and one on, and the Yankees were leading 4-3. When George calmly hit a home run, Yankee manager Billy Martin leapt from the dugout and protested: the tar on George's bat extended farther than the legal 18 inches (46 cm) from the bottom. The umpire measured the bat against home plate, which is 17 inches (43 cm) across. Yep, too much pine tar, said he, so no homer. George went berserk. The Royals filed a protest and the game was stopped. After some high-level bickering and dickering, George got his home run back (a decision that still makes umpires fume), and 25 days later the game was continued. Final score Royals 5, Yankees 4.

BATTLE DRESS

"We used no mattress on our hands,
No cage upon our face.
We stood right up and caught the ball
With courage and with grace."

So wrote catcher George Ellard about the 1869 Cincinnati Red Stockings. Back then, playing ball barehanded (and barefaced) was considered manly. So were broken fingers, fractured thumbs, sprained wrists, and bruised knuckles. Al Spalding wore kid gloves in 1877 while filling in at first base for the Red Stockings, but they didn't help much. In 1883, however, Providence shortstop Art Irwin (born in Toronto, died in mid-Atlantic when he jumped from an ocean liner) broke two fingers on his left hand. To protect them, he had a glovemaker devise a padded driving glove, a couple of sizes too big, with the third and fourth fingers sewn together. The bare hand disappeared.

Then in 1920, Cardinals pitcher Bill Doak thought of a way to make catching the ball easier. Lace the pocket between the thumb and first finger of the glove, and you not only protect the hand, you trap the ball.

Gloves come in many sizes, styles, and colors, but there are rules. A pitcher's glove must be all one color, but neither white nor gray, lest the ball be too hard to see. A catcher's glove can't be more than 38 inches (96.5 cm) around and a first baseman's glove can be a little larger than those of the other infielders. Infielders' gloves are smaller than outfielders' (the second baseman's is the smallest) to get rid of the ball fast.

History hand-in-glove (top to bottom): Fingerless glove, 1875; padded glove, about 1910; early model of a laced glove; and a modern fielder's glove.

18

The batting helmet, tried first in the early 1900s, and again by the Dodgers in 1941, wasn't made a rule until 51 years after the only death on a major league diamond. On August 16, 1920, Cleveland shortstop Ray Chapman stepped into the batter's box to face Yankee pitcher Carl Mays. Mays didn't like batters crowding the plate, which was what Chapman always did. Mays' third pitch was high and tight. A sickening crack echoed through the Polo Grounds. The ball bounced towards Mays, who picked it up to throw to first base. Then he saw Chapman fall into the arms of catcher Muddy Ruel — the ball had struck Chapman in the head, and he died early the next morning after surgery. He was 29 years old.

Indians outfielder Jimmy Piersall may have been the first to wear a helmet with earflaps, which are now required. After hitting two home runs in a game against Detroit in 1960, he clowned around a little. The Tiger pitcher was not amused, and Piersall knew his next at-bat might be hazardous to his head. He grabbed a Little Leaguer's helmet, with earflaps. He lived to clown around another day.

Foul Balls

The ball that hit Ray Chapman — in the fifth inning, as late afternoon shadows were lengthening — was scuffed and dirty. A sportswriter suggested that perhaps Ray couldn't see it very well. Ever since, umpires have been quick to replace soiled baseballs.

NO-FLAP, ONE-FLAP, TWO-FLAP RAP

On August 18, 1967, 22-year-old Red Sox slugger Tony Conigliaro was hit in the face by a pitch from Angel Jack Hamilton. It broke his cheekbone, ruined his vision, and wrecked his career. It also led to Rule 1.16, which made earflaps compulsory. Most helmets in the majors have one earflap, to protect the side of the head facing the pitcher. Switch-hitters — players who can bat from both sides of the plate — usually own two helmets, although a few wear a two-flapped model. On the field, no-flap helmets are worn backwards by catchers, and frontwards by Toronto first baseman John Olerud, who had brain surgery just before he turned pro.

The Tools of Ignorance

The catcher has more protection than any other player: in his helmet, mask, throat flap, chest protector, shinguards (reinforced with metal), he squats behind the plate like a giant armadillo — except his brain is bigger. The mask was invented after Harvard coach Fred Thayer decided his "receiver" should stand right behind home plate, rather than the customary 10 feet (3 m) back, to keep an eye on base runners. Catcher James Tyng, a handsome fellow, didn't want his face rearranged. A local tinsmith replaced the mesh from a fencing mask with curved iron bars, and Tyng's "bird-cage" mask entered the game on April 12, 1877, against the Massachusetts Live Oaks. Writers and spectators jeered. Catchers didn't, and we haven't seen their faces since.

Roger Bresnahan, a catcher with the New York Giants, invented shinguards and wore them first on September 24, 1908. Then made of padded leather, shinguards are now molded plastic with thin metal reinforcing strips. Flaps cover the knees and shoetops, to protect against spiking.

The catcher's gear is known as "the tools of ignorance," which means, according to many, that "only an idiot would be a catcher." The phrase may have been coined by Yankee catcher Herold Dominic "Muddy" Ruel, a highly educated lawyer who preferred diamonds to courtrooms and whose arms cradled the dying Ray Chapman.

DRESSED TO THE NINES — THE UNIFORM

Picture the pear-shaped powerhouse Kirby Puckett at the plate. Got it? Okay. Now picture this: Kirby's wearing canvas shoes, navy blue trousers held up by a woven cloth belt, a long-sleeved white shirt with a high stiff collar, a floppy silk tie, and a straw hat.

Such was the first baseball team uniform. When the 1849 New York Knickerbockers took the field, they looked like they might take tea, too. They were gentlemen. They

From silk tie to stretch pants

— 1850

didn't get dirty. They didn't spit. They didn't even get paid.

Twenty years later, the Cincinnati Red Stockings pulled on knee breeches and long scarlet socks. Then they pulled off 60 straight wins. (The owner's name was Champion — honest!) Every team in North America promptly ordered knickers and stockings.

The high collar and long sleeves gradually disappeared, the straw hat gave way to the billed cap (like a painter's or a porter's), and by 1900 or so a baseball uniform looked much like it does today — except it wasn't $125 worth of double-knit polyester, just $5 worth of wool. In 1910 a boy could buy a "baseball suit" for 98 cents. Those early uniforms were big and baggy, partly to allow for shrinkage. Sometimes it was hard to tell a shortstop from a low-lying cloud.

During the winter meetings of 1881 the owners decreed that each team would wear color-coded stockings. Baseball went color-mad for a while. In 1882 each starting player wore a different colored uniform: the pitcher wore light blue, the first baseman red and white, the shortstop maroon, the second baseman orange and blue, and the third baseman blue and white. The outfielders blossomed in white, gray, and red and black stripes. The catcher was eye-catching in crimson. Bench (substitute) players wore green and brown. The playing field became a flower garden, a rainbow, a fruit salad — a mess. After three months, the idea palled. (Or perhaps paled.)

Color, however, was in the game to stay. The 1901 Baltimore Orioles wore pink caps, black shirts bearing a huge yellow "O" over the heart, extra-roomy black knickers with yellow belts, and short jackets with two rows of pearl buttons.

Another brief experiment had the squads in short pants. The immediate result was short tempers, green knees, and red faces. Modesty soon

— 1870

— 1890

Negro League uniforms — about 1920

prevailed and the fellows covered their legs.

The feet at the ends of those legs wear two pairs of socks: plain white cotton socks, soon called "sanitary socks," and colored stirrup socks — sock tops attached to a skinny elastic strip that goes under the foot. The stirrup sock is a leftover from the days when each team wore different-colored stockings, a little piece of baseball history.

The two-sock tradition might never have begun without Napoleon "Nap" Lajoie, manager and second baseman for Cleveland in the 1900s. The team was named the Naps in his honor. (They didn't become "Indians" until four team-names later.) Lajoie was superb at the plate: one year he hit .426, the American League record, and his lifetime batting average was a healthy .338. He also swiped 381 bases during his career.

But that career was very nearly cut short in 1905. Playing second base can be dangerous, as Nap found out when he was badly spiked by a sliding runner. (This may have been revenge: the Naps sharpened their spikes with files before important games, in full view of their opponents.) The blue dye from Nap's stocking seeped into the wound and gave him a nasty case of blood poisoning. From then on, he wore white stockings under his blue stockings, and the stirrup sock was born.

One for the Road

Players wear white uniforms in their home park, and (usually) gray ones away from home. How come? Blame it on Cornelius McGillicuddy. "Connie Mack" ran the Philadelphia Athletics from 1901 to 1950, winning eight American League pennants and five World Series. One day "Mr. Mack," as he was called by everyone including his family, noticed that his team played hard in home games, leaping and diving and sliding and happy to hit the dirt. On the road, however, they goofed off. Mr. Mack figured that, with no washing machines handy, the players didn't want to get their pretty white uniforms dirty. He ordered a batch of gray uniforms and on the next road trip the team won six in a row.

Duds on the diamond

— *1930-1950*

— *the modern uniform*

Playing by the Numbers

When the notion of color-coding the players failed, the baseball brains decided to use numbers. The players grumbled. They weren't cops. They weren't convicts. Why should they wear numbers? But in 1929, Yankee Babe Ruth put a big "3" on his back and Lou Gehrig sported a "4" — the numerals decided by the batting order. Now numbers are a must: Official Baseball Rule No 1.11A says so.

Modern ballplayers can often pick their numbers. Numbers 50 and higher are given to new guys at spring training, so most rookies who make the team get rid of them fast. (Fireballing Blue Jay pitcher Juan Guzman kept number 66, convinced it helped him make the team.) Knuckleball pitchers — those masters of the mesmerizing floater — seem to favor number 49. It's on the backs of Tom Candiotti, Charlie Hough, and young Tim Wakefield. It's to honor the great number 49, knuckleballer Wilbur Wood, who pitched 88 games in 1968 and posted an ERA of 1.87.

Brian McRae, ace centerfielder with the Kansas City Royals, wanted number 11. It had been worn by his dad, Hal McRae, longtime designated hitter for the Royals and later its manager. A teammate already had 11, so Brian picked 56: add the two digits and you get 11. Outfielder Carlos May, whose birthday is May 17, picked number 17. The back of his uniform read "May 17."

Triskaidekaphobia

Roger Craig pitched for the 1962 New York Mets — probably the worst team ever. He lost 15 games in a row and tried to change his luck by changing his number — to 13. He lost again, 15-2, a difference of 13 runs.

The 1990 Boston Red Sox were in such a slump they turned to voodoo. The team moaned nonsense syllables sitting around 69 candles, a handful of fake snakes and spiders, two black cats, one rooster, and a uniform jersey with number 13 on the back. They also lost the next game.

MIDGET DIGIT

Bill Veeck, the man who first added names to the numbers on uniforms, was famous for bizarre stunts. When he managed the St. Louis Browns, he hired a 26-year-old player named Eddie Gaedel, who was 3 feet 7 inches (109 cm) tall. Eddie took his batting stance (which shrank his strike zone to about $1\frac{1}{2}$ inches or 3.8 cm), watched four pitches go over his head, and trotted down to first base. His number? $\frac{1}{8}$.

3RD INNING AT THE BALLPARK

"If you build it, he will come."

Shoeless Joe
W.P. Kinsella, 1982

FROM SKY TO SKYDOME

Let's travel back to May 15, 1862, when the first true baseball park opens for business. A couple of thousand fans in Brooklyn spend a dime each to sit on rough planks under a bright afternoon sky. Barriers around the field keep out the freeloaders.

The infield in that first baseball park looks familiar: there's the "diamond," which is really a square; the three bases and home plate set 90 feet (27.4 m) apart on the corners; the batter's box, the foul lines, the backstop. But the pitcher stands in a box just 45 feet (13.7 m) from the batter; and the catcher is three yards (2.7 m) behind the batter. Home plate is a white marble square, the bases are sacks full of sand, and the bullpen is a roped-off area for fans who couldn't get seats.

The rule-makers eventually settled on what we have today: the pitcher stands 60 feet, 6 inches (18.4 m) from the batter, one foot on a rubber slab, on a dirt mound 10 inches (26 cm) above field level; the catcher crouches right behind the batter; home plate is a rubber pentagon; and the bases are 15-inch (38 cm) squares of canvas filled with foam rubber on a metal plate, much like a deep-dish pizza. And in the bullpen, you'll find not "three-for-a-quarter" fans, but three-million-dollar-a-year relief pitchers.

Why the Pitcher Stands Where He Does

Amos Rusie, "The Hoosier Thunderbolt," pitched for the New York Giants. From 1890 to 1892, he struck out 985 batters. Because of guys like Amos, the pitcher's box was moved 15 feet, 6 inches (4.7 m) back to its present location. The Hoosier Thunderbolt's strikeouts dropped to 200 a year and opponents' batting averages soared.

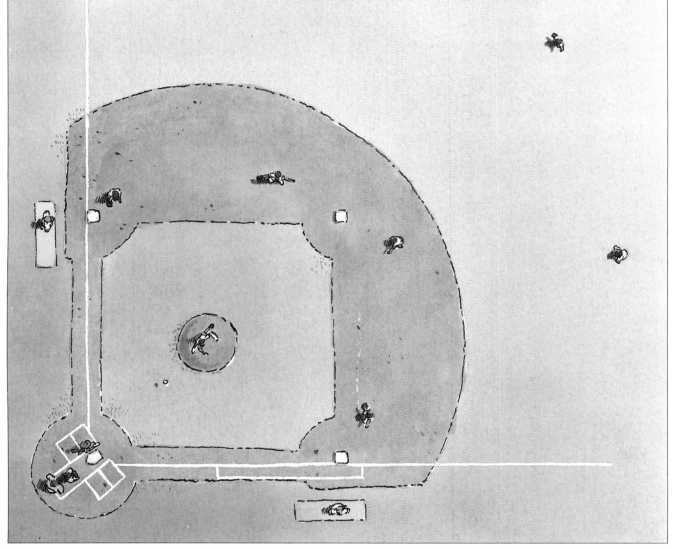

In 1958, minimum distances for the outfield were written into the rule book: 325 feet (99 m) for left and right fields, 400 feet (121.9 m) for center field. (Older parks with shorter fences, like Boston's Fenway, were allowed to keep them.) Before 1958, owners shaped their parks to help their teams win. Until its 1976 renovation, Yankee Stadium, which saw its first game on April 18, 1923, was called "The House that Ruth Built" for a good reason: left-handed Babe usually hit to the right — so the right-field fence was an easy 296 feet (90 m) away. Center field, at 490 feet (149 m), was known as Death Valley, where enemy homers died like flies.

Built of concrete and metal (fires had destroyed too many wooden parks), with three decks of seats hung on huge columns so every fan felt close to the game, Yankee Stadium was the model for ballparks until the 1950s. Then some clever architects did away with columns and built bigger stadiums that could host football games, rock concerts, track meets, and tractor pulls, as well as baseball games. Now you could see the whole field, but you needed a telescope to see who was doing what.

The Astrodome in Houston was the first covered stadium, shielding players from Texas heat and rain and wind. The first indoor baseball game — and the first complaints — occurred on April 9, 1965. The dome was made of 4,596 panes of see-through plastic, and players lost fly balls in the glare. It got so bad the outfielders wore helmets. Tinting the panes killed the glare — and the grass. When dead brown grass gave way to dead green artificial turf, domes and turf were soon sprouting like mushrooms.

Yankee Stadium (at left) and Houston's Astrodome (below)

But the old-fashioned ballpark is making a comeback: Oriole Park at Camden Yards in Baltimore could be a sign of things to come. (It's old-fashioned except for the food. If you don't want hot dogs, peanuts, or Cracker Jack, you can buy crab soup, Caesar salad, and grilled swordfish.) The park is right downtown, about a home run away from Babe Ruth's father's bar. It has a backstop of chicken wire, raised bullpens so you can see the relief pitchers warming up, and an outfield full of nooks and crannies. There's real grass and real sun and real sky, and every seat is a good one. We may be going back to the future.

Toronto's SkyDome (above) and Baltimore's Camden Yards (right)

The Toronto SkyDome has the only fully retractable roof in major league ball. Computer-driven, a marvel of engineering, the roof opens and closes in 20 minutes flat. Five parks have artificial turf but no dome. Baseball purists carp about carpets, but rain drains better on turf. Turf has also put new zip in the zipper industry: SkyDome has eight miles (12.8 km) of zippers that get replaced every couple of years.

LET THERE BE LIGHT

The first night game in baseball was played in 1880. The lights flickered and dimmed by turns, and there were more errors than runs. Lights were turned on next in 1935 at Crosley Field in Cincinnati. Like most teams during the Great Depression, the Reds were starved for paying customers and hoped night games would bring in some cash. Chicago's Wrigley Field was the last to light up, on August 8, 1988.

Blackouts were common for years. In a Detroit-Washington game back in the 1950s, the power failed as the pitcher started his windup. A minute later the lights came back on. Every ballplayer lay flat on the ground — except the pitcher. He was the only one who knew where the ball was.

Now, despite an electricity bill of $500,000 a year per team, more games are played "under the lights" than in daylight, which is too bad. Kids have to do some heavy negotiating to see the late innings of a World Series game.

From Cardboard . . .

Way back when, a fellow with a pencil marked the runs on a piece of cardboard tacked to a fence. You couldn't see the score too well, but keeping it cost about a dime, including the pencil — and the fellow. As parks and crowds grew bigger, so did scoreboards, but human hands still put the numbers up. (Manual scoreboards can still be found at die-hard Wrigley Field, Fenway Park and Joe Robbie Stadium, home to the Florida Marlins.)

... To Videoboard

When lights came to the ballpark, they also came to the scoreboard. For $50,000 — the cost of an early electric scoreboard — runs, hits, and errors glowed in the dark.

Now most parks have "color matrix boards" — oversized videos that do a lot more than tell you the score: they give you the words to the national anthem (in case you've forgotten them); flash instant replays (but no close calls — umpires vetoed that idea, fearing they might look foolish); send birthday greetings and marriage proposals to fans and players; advertise everything from banks to franks; pump up the crowd; and show old baseball movies during rainouts. Toronto's SkyDome boasts the largest of the large screens. Its JumboTRON, run by 11 high-tech experts, is 33 feet by 115 feet (10 m by 35 m), big enough to build a house on. The price tag was a mere $18 million.

THE ROCKET'S RED GLARE, THE BOMBS BURSTING IN AIR...

White Sox manager Bill Veeck always did things with a bang. In 1960 he loaded the scoreboard at Comiskey Park with giant pinwheels, sky rockets, and Roman candles and set them off to celebrate a White Sox win, home run, or fancy play. Visiting teams hated it — Cleveland outfielder Jimmy Piersall fired a ball at it once — but everybody else loved it. Now fireworks come with the territory.

Ground Rule Troubles

Ground rules, the rules that apply in a particular park, are made by a home team and agreed to by the visiting team before the game.

Some rules apply everywhere. The runner gets two bases when the ball is thrown into the seats, the dugout, or over the fence, or when the ball lands in fair territory and bounces into the seats. The runner gets a home run if the ball caroms off a fielder's glove (or his head, as Texas outfielder Jose Canseco painfully learned in 1993) and into the seats without touching the ground.

Others are unique.

If a ball hits a speaker hanging from the roof of Houston's Astrodome, Minnesota's Metrodome, or Seattle's Kingdome, it's still in play — unless it bounces foul. (In Seattle, two balls hit a speaker and never came down. The ump called them strikes.)

If a ball gets stuck or lost in the ivy on the outfield wall at Chicago's Wrigley Field, the runner gets a double. If a fielder tries to dig it out, the runner takes as many bases as he can. (Roberto Clemente once dug out a paper cup and threw it towards the infield. It never got there.)

At Toronto's SkyDome a similar rule applies to balls jammed behind banners and team logos on the fences.

The ladder beside the 37-foot-high (11.2 m) "Green Monster," the left-field wall at Boston's Fenway Park, is "in play" — part of the playing field — and once gave Washington's Jim Lemon an inside-the-park home run.

At one time, the entire length of the 125-foot (38 m) flagpole in Detroit's Tiger Stadium was in play, as was the stack of groundskeepers' brooms and rakes in Cleveland.

Weird Ground Rule 1

Vice President Hubert Humphrey went to a World Series game in 1965. On the field in front of him sat a Secret Service agent. The teams agreed that if a ball hit the agent, it would still be in play.

Weird Ground Rule 2

In 1910, two teams played in a New Jersey ballpark whose outfield included a railway track. A power hitter came up with the bases loaded and launched the ball into the smokestack of a passing train. The umpire ruled it a grand slam.

PARK OR ARK ?

Ruse Crews

At Montreal's Olympic Stadium in 1985, some seals from a pre-game circus seemed to like the Big O better than the Big Top. It took the grounds crew nearly an hour to round them up. In Toronto's old Exhibition Stadium, Dave Winfield, then a Yankee, threw a ball to a ballboy. Its flight was stopped by a seagull walking on the grass. The gull keeled over dead. Winfield was arrested and charged with cruelty to animals. Released with an apology, Winfield commissioned a painting of a (live) gull, which later raised $30,000 in a charity auction. Another gull, flying over Fenway Park in 1947, dropped a dead fish at the feet of pitcher Ellis Kinder. He won the game. In 1976, bees invaded Cincinnati's Riverfront Stadium and swarmed around third base for half an hour; and in Toronto in 1990, millions of gnats descended through the open SkyDome roof. Nobody on the field could see, including the umpire. The roof was closed, the gnats dispersed, and the game went on.

Groundskeepers have a bag of tricks as well as a bundle of brooms. In the new Oriole Park the infield grass is kept long, to help star shortstop Cal Ripken Jr. reach every ball hit at him. During the Dodgers-Giants rivalry in the 1960s, the Giants' crew soaked the path from first to second base to slow down ace thief Maury Wills. The base path was called "Maury's Lake."

Sloping the basepaths when a good bunting team comes to town helps to make a bunted ball roll foul. And in Yankee Stadium, back in the days when fans wore white shirts even to ball games, the crew lowered a big gauzy green curtain in center field when the home team was at bat, so the hitters could better see the white ball. The curtain was raised when visitors batted. All they saw was a backdrop of blinding white shirts. Now the few parks that have center field seats either paint them black or cover them with dark cloth.

Question: Which team always plays in its home park on opening day?
Answer: The Cincinnati Reds, to honor them as the first professional baseball team.

Field of Drains?

Baltimore's Oriole Park at Camden Yards boasts Prescription Athletic Turf. PAT sounds as if it's made in a test tube, but it's real grass that grows on a peat and sand mix. Under it is a maze of pipes, to drain the rain and water the grass. PAT's also been put down at Mile-High Stadium in Denver, where the Colorado Rockies hang their helmets, and at Atlanta's Fulton County Stadium, the home of the Braves.

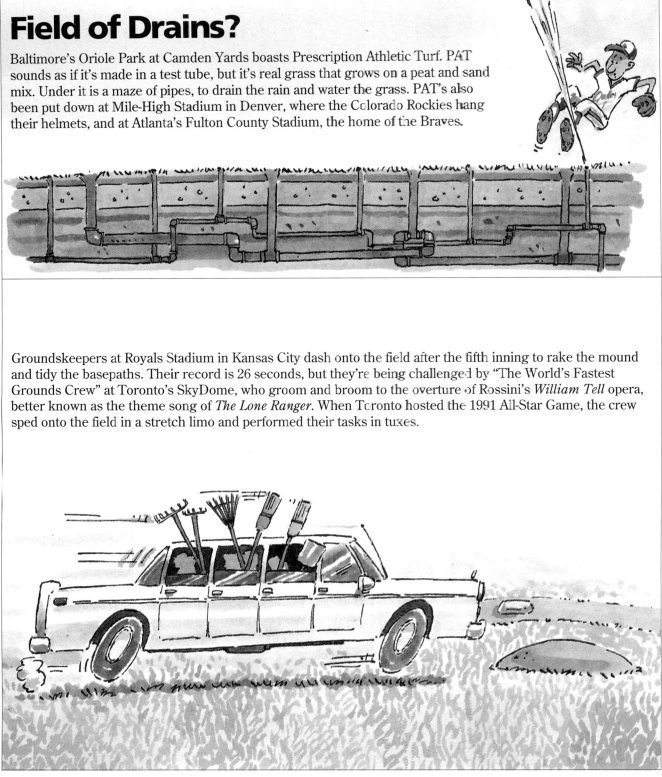

Groundskeepers at Royals Stadium in Kansas City dash onto the field after the fifth inning to rake the mound and tidy the basepaths. Their record is 26 seconds, but they're being challenged by "The World's Fastest Grounds Crew" at Toronto's SkyDome, who groom and broom to the overture of Rossini's *William Tell* opera, better known as the theme song of *The Lone Ranger*. When Toronto hosted the 1991 All-Star Game, the crew sped onto the field in a stretch limo and performed their tasks in tuxes.

4TH INNING

THE BATTER, THE PITCHER, THE UMPIRE

"Pitching is 75% of the game, and the other half is hitting."
Yogi Berra

THE BATTER

1. See ball.
2. Swing bat.
3. Hit ball.
4. Run.

Sounds easy, but it isn't. Hitting a small round ball with a skinny round stick is never easy, especially when the ball is speeding towards your body at 90 miles (144 km) an hour. Pretend you're at the plate. The pitch will take a half-second to reach you. In that half-second you must focus on the ball, figure out what kind of pitch it is, judge whether it's a ball or a strike, and swing — or not swing — the bat. (You might also duck, jump, or fall down — or you'll be given first base or first aid. Maybe both.) No wonder even the best batters get only three hits for every 10 times at bat.

Short Story

Wee Willie Keeler, one of the all-time great hitters, summed it all up, short and sweet: "Hit 'em where they ain't," that is, hit the ball where a fielder can't catch it. Five feet four inches and 140 lbs. (1.6 m and 63.5 kg), Willie hit only 34 home runs in 19 years, but his lifetime batting average was .341. In 1897, playing for Baltimore, he got 239 hits in 129 games, a .424 average, with the shortest bat ever used in pro ball, a 30½ inch (77.5 cm) toothpick.

The Hit List

Some hits come from skill, some are plain luck, but the greater your skill, the luckier you get. Here are some of the hits skill and luck can put together.

Baltimore chop

The ball hits the ground near home plate and bounds high over the heads of the pitcher and infielders. Perfected by Wee Willie Keeler of the 1890s Baltimore Orioles, whose home infield was kept hard, it's now a favorite on bouncy artificial turf.

Bloop, blooper

A poorly hit ball falls too far back for the infielders, but not far enough for the outfielders to catch. Pitcher Jim Brosnan said the sound it makes is that "of a soft tomato struck with a broomstick." Also called a drooper, a looper, a pooper, a plunker, a punker, a bleeder, a stinker, a sucker, a squibber, and a Texas Leaguer (in honor of the inexperienced hitters in that minor league).

Broken-bat hit/single

A ball is hit off the skinny part of the bat and snaps the bat in two. (Or a ball hit off Jim Abbott: in a 1992 game against the Blue Jays, Abbott's pitches broke eight bats.) While everyone's watching the ball, the bits of bat can be lethal weapons. In August 1978, Dodger catcher Steve Yeager was in the on-deck circle when a splinter from a broken bat pierced his throat. The team doctor kept Steve from bleeding to death.

Dying quail, seagull, or swan

The hit ball drops suddenly to earth in an unexpected place, the way a shot bird might. A strong wind blowing in helps.

Line drive, liner

The ball travels fast in a straight line, rather than an arc; known also as a "frozen rope." A low line drive is also called a "clothesline" or a "blue dart."

Opposite field hit

Yup, just what you think it is. Many batters are "pull" hitters: they swing a little too soon. This pulls the ball to the left for a right-handed hitter, to the right for a lefty. If you can hit safely and often to the opposite field, righty to right, lefty to left, you'll be laughing all the way to first base — and the bank.

THE BUNT

In 1866 Dickey Pearce, a short shortstop — an inch (2.5 cm) shorter than Wee Willie Keeler — with the Brooklyn Atlantics, slid one hand along his bat, faced the pitcher, nudged the ball a few feet — and ran like heck to first base. Dickey had just dropped the first bunt. The infielders stared at it, then swore at it. They still do. Wee Willie was a master of the bunt; so were Ty Cobb and Jackie Robinson. So are Jay Bell and Felix Fermin.

When do you bunt? When the manager tells you to. Usually that's when a runner's on first, and you want to move him into scoring position (second or third base), even if you're put out doing it. When the infielder rushes in to scoop up the ball, the runner takes off for the next base. This is a sacrifice bunt. Then there's the squeeze bunt. That's when you want a runner on third base to score. In the "safety squeeze," the runner waits to see if it's a good bunt. In the "suicide squeeze," the runner takes off from third base as soon as the ball leaves the pitcher's hand. If the batter doesn't hit, the runner's dead at the plate.

A BET ON A BUNT

During his minor-league years, catcher Yogi Berra had a terrible time fielding bunts. Finally his manager bet him a steak dinner that he couldn't throw out one runner at first base in an entire game. Yogi was as bad as usual. Then he came up to bat. He dropped a bunt right in front of the plate, pounced on the ball, and tossed it to first base. He threw himself out, but he won the bet.

THE PITCHER

Pitching is the heart of baseball. Alone on the raised mound, the pitcher takes on all comers. It's always High Noon at the ballpark.

In the early days, it was the pitcher's job to throw the ball so that it could be hit. He wasn't allowed to throw overhand, and the batter could insist that the ball be thrown high or low.

In the 1880s the rules changed. The pitcher no longer served the batter, he challenged him. It's been a see-saw battle ever since, with batters getting the edge through changes in the strike zone and the distance and height of the pitcher's mound, with pitchers taking that edge away with speed, cunning, and an array of pitches the early throwers never dreamed of.

Which Pitch Is Which?

There are three basic pitches: the fastball, the curveball, and the change-up, which is just a slower version of either. But pitchers have perfected dozens of other pitches to fool batters, using different arm and wrist motions, different grips — and cheating. Here's a sample handful of these pitches.

Slider

Once known as "the nickel curve," the slider is a curveball that slides out of the fingers, as if you're throwing a football. Where a curveball has forward spin and can drop more than a foot (30 cm), the slider has side spin and drops about five inches (12 cm). Steve Carlton was a master.

Forkball

The ball is held in the "fork" of the index and second fingers. When you throw it hard, it drops suddenly at the plate.

Screwball

The ball is let go with an outward snap of the wrist. Thrown by a right-hander, it breaks down and in to a right-handed batter, down and away from a lefty; thrown by a left-hander, it breaks down and in to a lefty, down and away from a righty. Hall of Fame pitcher Christy Mathewson called it his "fadeaway."

Knuckleball

The ball is held against the knuckles, fingertips, or more commonly the fingernails and pitched slowly, without any spin. At the mercy of air currents, it floats and wobbles and dips. The knuckleball is easy on the arm (knuckleballers often pitch until they're 45 or older) but it's hard to hit and hard to catch.

One batter said that trying to hit Phil Niekro's knuckleball was like trying to eat Jell-O with chopsticks. Niekro's catcher, Bob Uecker, claimed that the best way to handle it was to wait for it to stop rolling and then pick it up.

Eephus

Also called gondola, balloon, lob, parachute, and ridiculous. There's no rule about the arc of a pitch, so in 1943 Pittsburgh's Rip Sewell threw a ball 25 feet (7.6 m) in the air, which eventually floated to earth in front of a baffled batter. It continued to baffle batters until 1946, when Ted Williams, the greatest hitter next to Babe Ruth, hit an eephus out of the park in the All-Star game. (Note: the word "eephus" means absolutely nothing.)

Clamshells, Corncobs, and Curveballs

William Cummings, nicknamed "Candy," threw the first curveball in 1863 — using a clamshell. He got the idea of the curveball from throwing clamshells while he was at boarding school. Shaped as they are, they naturally curved. Candy made clamshells veer right and then left and went on to throw curves (and madden hitters) for the Brooklyn Excelsiors. But the Waner brothers, Paul and Lloyd, Pittsburgh outfielders during the 1940s, could hit any curveball. As boys they practised by hitting corncobs. Paul claimed there were more curves in the corncob games than he ever saw in real games, and there was motivation, too. If you didn't hit the corncob, it would hit you — hard.

PAIGE PITCH TOSSED OUT

Leroy Paige (known as "Satchel" from his job carrying suitcases at age seven) was one of the greatest pitchers in history. He had a 37-year career, 20 years in the Negro Leagues and 17 in the majors — and he was 59 when he pitched his last game in 1965. (He gave up one hit.) He had a snapping fastball that he called his "be ball" ("because it be where I want it to be"), and a hopper that jumped six inches (15 cm). His famous "hesitation pitch" involved pausing just before throwing the ball. He learned it as a boy throwing rocks, tricking the other kids into ducking too soon. The pitch was so good it was banned. "I had the batters swinging when I still had the ball in my hand," Satchel said. His advice to pitchers still says it all: "Throw strikes. Home plate don't move."

oy "Satchel" Paige

Spin Doctors

Since baseball began, pitchers have tried to alter — or "doctor" — the ball to fool the batters. The spitball — moistened with tobacco juice, saliva, sweat, oil, wax, or Vaseline — slipped off the pitcher's fingers easily, cut down spin, and dropped sharply and steeply when it reached the plate. It probably disgusted the catcher, but it worked. Spitballer Ed Walsh of the Chicago White Sox retired in 1917 with the lowest career ERA in baseball history: 1.82.

Another popular trick was the scuffball. The ball's surface is roughened on one side by sandpaper, dirt, a belt buckle, phonograph needles, spikes — even a nutmeg grater. When the pitcher throws it, the ball meets more air resistance on the scuffed side, so it swerves in that direction.

Both pitches were made illegal in 1920, but pitchers already using the spitball, including the fellow with a name like a rock group — Urban Shocker — were allowed to continue until they retired. In spite of suspensions and fines — and TV closeups — pitchers still try to doctor the ball. On June 22, 1992, Yankee pitcher Tim Leary was accused by Baltimore batters of scuffing the ball, and millions of TV viewers saw him slip something in his mouth when the umpire approached. At the end of the inning, he spit something out as he left the field.

Question: Why is the pitcher 60 feet, 6 inches (18.4 m) from the batter?
Answer: Because the fellow who drew the diagram back in 1893 had messy handwriting. He wrote 60' 0", but his 0 looked like a 6.

THE MAN BEHIND THE MAN BEHIND THE BATTER: THE UMPIRE

Alexander Cartwright had written the rules, but who would enforce them? Baseball needed an umpire. Enter William Wheaton, wealthy and distinguished New York lawyer. Wearing a top hat, a Prince Albert coat, and kid gloves, he strolled behind the foul line near first base, sat on a stool, cane in hand — and the first recorded game of baseball in the United States was underway.

First recorded game — October 6, 1845

Most early umpires were rich and respected gentlemen, leaders in business and society. Some stood behind the pitcher or beside the batter; some knelt along the first base line. A few relaxed in rocking chairs 20 feet (6 m) behind home plate. There was no training, no dress code, and no money — just the honor of being "the sole judge of fair and unfair play."

When players went professional, so did umpires. In 1879 (the year you drew a walk after nine balls) the National League appointed a group of 20 men from which a team could pick an umpire — and pay him $5 a game. A few seasons later, the American Association, a professional league that existed from 1882 to 1891, hired and paid umpires $140 a month and told them which games they'd judge. They were also told to wear blue flannel coats and caps — the "men in blue" had arrived.

Umpiring was now no job for gentlemen. In fact, it was downright dangerous. Umpires were kicked, cursed, spiked, and spat upon by players. Managers threatened and screamed, just like today. Fans threw bottles, cans, and even rocks. In 1907, one of the smartest (college degree), youngest (first pro job at 22), and toughest (amateur boxer) umpires, Billy Evans, was hit in the head by a bottle thrown by a Cardinals fan.

His skull was fractured and he almost died. In 1921, he was challenged to a fight by all-time great hitter and all-time mean dude Ty Cobb. They met under the grandstand after the game. Billy unloaded a couple of left hooks, then stood over the dazed Cobb and called him out.

When catchers donned masks and chest pads to ward off wild pitches, foul tips, and flying bats, umpires did too. Until 1970, American League umpires wore the bulky awkward pad over their clothes. They couldn't bend too well — it's hard when you're wearing a mattress — so they tended to have a higher strike zone than their NL brothers, who wore a smaller pad under their shirts.

Soon the umpire became indispensable: no professional game could be played without one — two by 1920, three by 1933, four starting in 1952, and from 1948 on, six for all championship and World Series games. The umpire had all the power — to start a game, end a game, and make every decision in between, but not much of the cash. In 1968 umpires formed their own union. Three strikes in 15 years brought salary increases, paid vacations, and a pension plan. Minor league umps start at $400 a week, but in the Bigs, they can bank on $70,000 a year.

Each year, 500 people sign up at professional umpires' schools for a five-week course as tough as Marine boot camp. Fewer than 50 land jobs in the minor leagues. After 10 years or so, a handful of those may make it to the 62-man major-league umpiring roster. It's a hard climb to the top.

It's even harder if you're black, Hispanic, or female. Not until 1966 — 19 years after Jackie Robinson broke the color bar — was a black umpire elevated to the major leagues. It took another eight years for the first Hispanic-American to don the blue. And women? Forget it. Pam Postema stood 17th out of 100 at umpire school, put up with terrible abuse for 13 years in the minors, working more than 2,000 games — and then baseball said, "Go away." She's filed a sex discrimination suit in the U.S. Supreme Court,

Pam Postema

but the hurt is so deep, she can't bear to watch a ball game. Umpiring, like baseball itself, still has a long way to go.

Cub Stub Brings Broom Doom,
or,
Why Umpires Use a Whisk

Early umpires swept home plate with an ordinary long-handled broom which they'd then throw in the general direction of the visitors' dugout. In 1904, a Chicago Cub running from third to home stepped on the umpire's broom and wrecked his ankle. The word went out: the umpire's broom had to fit in his pocket.

KILL THE NUMP!
The Case of the Wandering "n"

"Umpire" comes from the old French word "noumpere" (non-peer, not an equal, one who decides disputes between equals). When it traveled to England, it lost its "n" and appeared in a 1400 edition of Aesop's Fables as "oumpere," soon spelled "umpire" — just as a napron became an apron, a nadder became an adder, and an ewt became a newt.

Match Point

Bob Emslie, a gifted umpire and one of the few Canadians in the game, was once called a "blind robber" by hot-tempered John McGraw, manager of the New York Giants. The next day, Bob came to the park with a rifle. He split a match, poked a dime into it, and stuck it in the ground near second base. He walked back to home plate, turned, and fired. The dime sailed into center field. McGraw never again made a crack about Bob's vision.

Why the Umpire Points a Finger and Makes a Fist

The first umpires called balls and strikes simply by saying the words. But William "Dummy" Hoy — he insisted on the nickname — changed all that. After spinal meningitis at age two, Hoy could neither hear nor speak. He grew up to be a skillful batter and a star center fielder. (He had a 14-season average of .288, 597 stolen bases, and, with an arm like a high-powered rifle, 3,959 put-outs.) But Hoy had to read the umpire's lips to know whether the last pitch was a ball or a strike. When big-league pitchers started "quick-pitching" him, his timing was ruined, and his batting average plummeted. Dummy asked his third-base coach for help: one sign for a strike, another for a ball. It worked. The following season, in 1887, he batted .367 and his team won the pennant. Umpires liked the idea of hand signals, and they've been part of the game ever since.

5TH INNING

THE RUNNER, THE FIELDER, THE CATCHER

"He's like a little kid in a train station. You turn your back on him and he's gone."
Pitcher Doc Medich, about Rickey Henderson

THE RUNNER

It's good to be speedy, but it's better to be smart — and it helps to be tricky, too.

The basic idea is simple enough: hit the ball into fair territory and run. If it doesn't get caught, you can run all the way back to where you started — and put a run on the scoreboard.

Sometimes it's not that simple. Mainly because of rules like these:

1. **Only one runner can occupy a base.**

   In the 1963 World Series, two Dodgers ended up on third base together. Yankee shortstop Tony Kubek ran over with the ball, tagged everybody in sight including the umpire, and said: "One of you guys is out." He was right.

   In a 1920s game, *three* Dodgers landed on third base. Two were out for breaking the rule, and the other was tagged out trying to run back to second. End of inning.

2. **A runner is out if he passes the runner ahead of him.**

   After he hit a home run with a runner on base, Yankee Lou Gehrig forgot this rule. It cost him the 1931 home-run title.

44

3. A runner must touch all the bases.

Tell that to Fred Merkle. It was the bottom of the ninth in the 1908 pennant race between the New York Giants and the Chicago Cubs. New York was at bat with two out. A runner was on third and Fred Merkle was on first. The score was tied 1-1. The batter looped a single into center field and the man on third scored the winning run. Fred cheered with everybody else — and ran off the field. But he had forgotten to touch second base — the play wasn't completed and he wasn't officially "safe." The Cubs appealed, the game was replayed, and New York lost the game and the pennant. Fred Merkle won a nickname — "Bonehead."

4. A runner must touch the bases in order.

This rule was made in 1920, after a game in which the Philadelphia Athletics had runners on first and third. The manager flashed the sign for a double steal. The man on first stole second, but the man on third didn't move. So the runner on second ran back to first and stole second again. The catcher threw to second — and the runner on third ran home to score.

The strangest example of bad base-running occurred in 1883, when a bewildered batter finally got a hit. Overcome with excitement, he took off — for third base. With everyone yelling what he thought was encouragement, he kept on running — to second, to first, and home. He was called out.

5. A runner can't <u>intentionally</u> interfere with a batted ball or a fielder trying to field the ball, and no run can score as a result of the interference.

Officially Rule 7.09h, it's called the "Jackie Robinson rule." Robinson wrecked dozens of double plays by letting the ball hit him as he ran to second. He'd be out, but the batter would reach first base. In the 1978 World Series, Yankee Reggie Jackson pulled the same trick: he stuck out his hip, the ball bounced into right field, the batter was safe on first, and a run scored. The umpire ruled that Reggie didn't mean to get in the way. The Yankees won the game 4-3, and went on to win the Series.

COOL PAPA BELL "THE FASTEST MAN ON SPIKES"

Negro League star James Bell could fly around the bases. (He was no slouch with the bat, either. In 1946, at age 43, his average was .411.) He once scored from second base on a fly ball, and from first on a sacrifice bunt — when he was 45 years old. Satchel Paige said that Bell was so fast "he can switch off the light and jump into bed before the room gets dark."

Slide Show

In baseball, inches can mean the difference between "safe" and "out." Touching the bag with just your hand or foot makes a small target — there's not much of you there to be tagged.

Mike "King" Kelly started it all. Playing for Cincinnati and Chicago in the 1880s, Kelly perfected the feet-first slide and invented the hook slide. (The base is hooked by one leg, while the rest of you is as far away from the baseman as it can be.) He also made the stolen base a thing of beauty as well as an everyday weapon. Back then stealing was rare, but Kelly swiped 368 bases. Handsome, dashing, adored by fans, King Kelly was the first player besieged for autographs. He often rode to the park in formal dress and silk hat, in a carriage drawn by white horses. He even had a song written for him, "Slide, Kelly, Slide."

The head-first slide, exciting and risky, came with helmets and sliding gloves. Pete Rose — always ready to take a gamble — raised it to a fine art. It's faster than the feet-first slide, especially when diving back to a base to avoid getting picked off. But it's downright dangerous at home plate, where the catcher blocks the way like a Sherman tank and the plate is hard, not like the pillowy bases. Another Kelly, Blue Jays third baseman Kelly Gruber, found this out in 1992, when his chin hit the plate and he knocked himself silly.

Excuses: Inkin', Drinkin', and Odd...

Some players don't slide when they should, and get tagged out. Babe Ruth never slid at exhibition games: His Nibs didn't want to disappoint autograph-seekers by breaking the pen in his back pocket. Many early players didn't want to dent their hip flasks of liquor. Charles "Casey" Stengel, off-the-wall manager of the Dodgers, the Yankees, and the "Amazin' Mets," was booed for not sliding when he played for Pittsburgh in 1918. He faced the fans and yelled: "With the salary I'm getting, I'm so hollow and starving, I'm liable to explode like a light bulb!"

Great Diamond Robberies

The phrase "base-stealing" showed up in a New York paper in 1862, although no records were kept until 1886. (The first "sliding steal" took place in 1865, by Eddie Cuthbert of the Philadelphia Keystones.) The stolen base grew in importance all through the "dead ball era," right up until 1920, when Babe Ruth and the home run launched the "lively ball" era and changed the game. Thirty years passed before base-stealing became a powerful weapon again. Among the best base bandits were Jackie Robinson, Willie Mays, and Luis Aparicio. If Luis got a single, it was declared an "Aparicio double," because you could bet a month's allowance he'd end up on second base.

Jackie Robinson

The greatest thief of the early years was Tyrus Raymond Cobb, the first player elected to the Hall of Fame. His gentle nickname, "The Georgia Peach," is puzzling: Ty Cobb was a mean, vicious, selfish, racist bully, who spiked players just for the fun of it. (Only three baseball people showed up at his funeral in 1961.) But Ty was a magnificent ballplayer. He practiced bunting by putting his sweater on the infield and making the ball stop on its sleeve. Once he reached first base, you could put a run up on the scoreboard. One confused catcher said, "The only way to make a play on Cobb is to throw to the base ahead of the one he's trying to steal — at least he won't get any farther."

Willie Mays

His 1915 major league record of 96 stolen bases stood until 1962, when Maury Wills stole 106. Since then, such daring robbers as Lou Brock (118 in 1974), now teaching his larcenous trade to the Cardinals, and Rickey Henderson (130 in 1982 and still stealing) have outshone the early stars.

But Cobb's record for stealing home still stands. In his 23-year career he stole home 50 times, eight times in one season. He stole all the way from first to home four times. He even stole home in a World Series game.

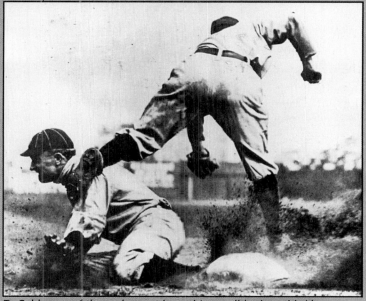
Ty Cobb, one of the early great base-thieves, slides into third base.

THE FIELDER

By the time fielders were called fielders (instead of "scouts"), in 1870, the baseball brains knew that "the best offense is a good defense." Good fielding wins games — even against burly sluggers.

The Infield

The first, second, and third basemen, and shortstop are the first line of that defense. An infield play is usually a sure out. Why? Because an amazing 49% of all fair batted balls are grounders — they hit the ground on the infield where infielders can get to them fast and throw the runners out.

If you're long, lean, and left-handed, like Chicago Cub Mark ("Amazing") Grace, you're a natural first baseman. Grace can reach throws that are high or wide, he can field bunts quickly, he can cover lots of ground between first and second, and he can tag the runner faster on a pick-off throw from the pitcher. (But short chunky right-handers like Pete Rose do okay, too.)

Second basemen and shortstops need the speed of a cheetah and the skills of an acrobat. They scoop up ground balls and turn most of the double plays. And they have to be nimble enough to evade a sliding runner intent on serious bodily harm. Robbie Alomar, who leaps and flips and dives like a dolphin, and shortstop Ozzie ("The Wizard of Oz") Smith, with a record 621 assists in getting runners out, are model infielders.

The third baseman lives in "the hot corner." He's got to have good range, a strong arm, and quick feet. It also takes a crazy kind of courage to dive to the turf for a ball shooting down the line, or to throw your body in front of a ball that's faster — and fatter — than a speeding bullet. Third-base aces Brooks Robinson and Mike Schmidt collected thousands of bruises in their careers — along with 26 Gold Gloves.

Pittsburgh shortstop John "Honus" Wagner — whose baseball card was bought in 1991 by Wayne Gretzky for $451,000, and sold in 1992 for half that — may have been the game's greatest shortstop. His hands were like shovels, and when he scooped up the ball, he'd throw half a pound of dirt with it. He claimed he once fielded a dog along with the ball and threw both to first base. Bowlegged and long-armed, he was said to tie his shoelaces without bending his knees. Honus was generous, kind, and easygoing, the opposite of Ty Cobb. In the 1907 World Series, Cobb reached first base and yelled to Wagner: "Watch out, Krauthead! I'm coming down!" Wagner tagged him out with such enthusiasm that several Cobb teeth were knocked loose. Wagner and the Pirates also took the Series.

On the Other Hand . . .

Then there was Henry "Zeke" Bonura, Chicago infielder in the 1930s, whose hands were all thumbs. With two out and the bases loaded, Zeke snared a grounder, dropped it, picked it up, dropped it, and then kicked it. By the time he'd recaptured it, three runs were in, and the batter was nearing third. Zeke threw the ball over, and it landed in the dugout. The batter scored.

Double Talk

(left to right) Tinker, Evers and Chance

The most renowned infielders — but not the best — to turn the double play were Chicago Cubs shortstop Joe Tinker, second baseman Johnny Evers, and first baseman-manager Frank Chance. (It was Evers who noticed Fred Merkle's bonehead play in the 1908 World Series, and quickly touched second.) All were rough, tough, talented, and ready to battle anybody, including one another. (Tinker and "Crab" Evers had a fight in 1905 about sharing a taxi to the ballpark and didn't speak to each other, on or off the field, for 22 years.) The three were elected as a unit, a one-time occurrence, to the Hall of Fame in 1946. Their names are linked forever, as in this verse written in 1910 by journalist and Giants fan Franklin P. Adams:

Baseball's Sad Lexicon

These are the saddest of possible words,
Tinker-to-Evers-to-Chance.
Trio of Bear Cubs fleeter than birds,
Tinker-to-Evers-to-Chance.
Ruthlessly pricking our gonfalon bubble,
Making a Giant hit into a double,
Words that are weighty with nothing but trouble.
Tinker-to-Evers-to-Chance.

Three-in-One Thrills

It's the fastest way to end an inning except for an earthquake or an invasion from outer space. The triple play is so rare that most fans have never seen one. Unassisted triple plays — when one player gets three outs — have happened only nine times in the majors. On October 10, 1920, Cleveland second baseman Bill Wambsganss (whose name means "goosebelly," which is a lot easier to spell) turned the only triple play in World Series history. With Dodgers on first and second, he caught a line drive for the first out, stepped on the bag for the second out, and tagged a runner for the third. The Indians won the Series. In the 1992 World Series, Toronto completed a triple play on Atlanta's Deion Sanders — but umpire Bob Davidson missed Kelly Gruber's tag. The next day the ump admitted he'd goofed — an event as rare as the triple play itself. Toronto won the Series anyway.

Hale Almost Ex-Hale in Heads-Up Play

In a Red Sox-Indian game back in 1935, with the bases loaded and nobody out, Boston's Joe Cronin came up to bat. He hammered a line drive right at Cleveland third baseman Odell Hale. The ball caromed off Hale's forehead into the glove of shortstop Billy Knickerbocker (really!). Billy threw it to second baseman Roy Hughes, who fired it to first for the strangest triple play in history.

Like Father, Like Son...

On May 11, 1993, Todd Hundley of the New York Mets hit into the first triple play of the season. Watching him was his father, Randy — who had hit into a triple play 21 years earlier.

BASE BEHAVIOR

The fake throw, the hidden ball, the pretend-you-have-the-ball-when-it's-out-in-left-field trick — all are used by wily basemen. Minnesota's Kent Hrbek raised trickery to new levels — literally — when he lifted a Blue Jay runner off first base and touched him with the ball. The umpire called the runner out, a "base" judgment indeed. But justice prevailed when Boston's Roger Clemens, who resembles a large tree, pushed Toronto's Alfredo Griffin, who's more like a shrub, right off first base. This time, the umpire refused to call Griffin out.

Back in the days before there were umpires at the bases, Baltimore third baseman John McGraw really knew how to hold runners on: he stopped them from scoring by grabbing them by the belt. But Pete Browning — the fellow who asked Bud Hillerich for the first Louisville Slugger — tricked the trickster: when he reached third, he secretly undid his belt buckle. A runnerless John gaped while a beltless Pete escaped — and scored.

The Outfield

The right, left, and center fielders are the last line of defense. An outfielder has to think fast, run fast, and throw fast — in that order. Before every pitch — and there might be 150 in a game — a *good* outfielder knows the answers to nine questions:

1. What's the score?
2. What inning is it?
3. How many are out?

   (If an outfielder can't answer these three questions, he soon seeks other employment.)

4. What pitch will the pitcher pitch?
5. Where are the other outfielders?
6. Where are the base-runners and how fast can they run?
7. Where will the batter hit the ball and how fast can he run?
8. Will the wind mess me up?
9. Will the sun mess me up?

If he gets the answers right, he "gets a good jump" and he's on the move before the ball is even hit.

The right fielder needs the strongest arm: a long accurate throw to third base or home plate can prevent a run. Detroit Tiger Al Kaline was just about perfect: he had an arm like a grenade launcher, played 133 games straight in 1971 without an error, and won 11 Gold Gloves.

Managers often use left field as a parking spot for players who are brilliant with the bat but lousy with the leather. Washington Senator Leon "Goose" Goslin is typical: for seven years in a row (1922-1928) he hit .300 or better, and in left field he impersonated a large lawn ornament. He'd take a gander at fly balls and remain unmoved, as the center fielder did his job.

Joe DiMaggio

After the pitcher, catcher, and shortstop, the center fielder is the most important man on the team. He's usually the best fielder and always the boss. More balls are hit to center than to left or right field, and it's up to him to call for a catch, or call off the other fielders. With the most ground to cover, he must be fast, with a strong arm to throw to third and home. Wall-climbing skills are handy, too: Spiderman would be terrific. Center fielders tend to

Devon White

be slim of build and long of leg, like Joe DiMaggio, Willie Mays, and Devon White. But Minnesota's Kirby Puckett, a five-foot-eight (1.7 m), 226-pound (102.5 kg) bowling pin with shoes, is a five-time Gold Glove winner, and an All-Star seven years in a row.

Kirby Puckett

Dog Grabs Pants, Wolf Grabs Chance

In an 1888 game, an outfielder was outsmarted — by a dog. Louisville's Chicken Wolf (real name William van Winkle Wolf) hit a single to right. Cincinnati's Abner Powell ran after the ball, but a sleeping dog woke up (in a fowl temper?) and ran after Abner. The dog hung on to his pantleg until Chicken Wolf scored.

THE CATCH

Willie Mays of the New York Giants could do it all: run, steal, hit, and field. He's been called the best center fielder in the game, and he showed it on September 29, 1954. It was the first game of the World Series, and the score was tied 2-2 in the top of the eighth. With runners on first and second and nobody out, Cleveland's Vic Wertz hammered the ball 440 feet (134 m) to deep center. Mays turned, dashed for the fence, made an over-the-shoulder catch, and rifled the ball back to the infield. The runner on second tagged up and ran to third — but that's as far as he got. The next two batters were outs. The Giants won the game and the Series. "The Catch" — capitalized immediately and still — won a spot in baseball history.

THE UNCATCH

Forty-two years before Willie Mays, another New York Giant center fielder made headlines. In the final game of the 1912 World Series, with his team leading 2-1 in the tenth and set to win the championship, Fred Snodgrass caught a fly ball from Boston's Clyde Engle. Then he dropped it. Engle went to second. Pitcher Christy Mathewson walked the next batter. Both came home to score and Boston won the Series. Fred died in 1974, when he was 87 — and nobody ever let him forget the three words that made him famous: "The Snodgrass Muff."

THE CATCHER

One hundred and fifty years ago the catcher was the fellow who kept the ball from hitting a fan in the face. Today he's the busiest guy on the field. The catcher is the onfield strategist — like the quarterback in football. He's also the last line of defense — like the goalie in hockey or soccer.

Would you apply for this job? You have to:

1. Put on and take off the "tools of ignorance" (see Second Inning) at least eight times a day.
2. Call the pitches — tell the pitcher what pitch to pitch, using hand signals.
3. Know each pitcher's strengths, weaknesses, and weird habits.
4. Know the same about enemy batters.
5. Deploy the defense — tell the fielders where to field.
6. Field bunts.
7. Catch pop flies.
8. Throw out runners trying to steal.
9. Back up first and third bases if there's no play at the plate.
10. Block all incoming balls — high, wide, low, and life-threatening.
11. Block all incoming runners — high, wide, low, and life-threatening.

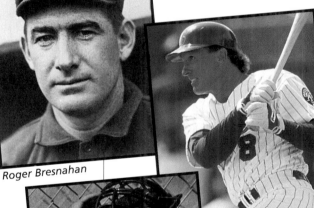

Roger Bresnahan

Buck Martinez

Gary Carter

The ideal catcher has a body like a refrigerator, an arm like a howitzer, and more memory than a computer. Skin like a rhino's helps, too: a catcher gets hurt — a lot. So it's no wonder good catchers are rare and enjoy — if that's the word — long careers. Carlton Fisk, who retired in 1993, leads the majors: he caught 2,226 games in 24 years. ("Pudge" Fisk also holds the record for catching the longest game: 25 innings, on May 8 *and* 9, 1984.) Gary Carter, lately of Montreal, racked up close to 2,100 games in a 19-year career. They're a hardy bunch — unless they break down or break bones. Roger Bresnahan, first to wear shinguards and first catcher in the Hall of Fame, played 139 games in 1908, wore out his knees, and was never again a full-time catcher. Buck Martinez, Toronto catcher in the 1980s, had his leg badly broken while blocking the plate against Seattle Mariner Phil Bradley. (Buck held onto the ball and Bradley was out.) When Buck retired, he got another break: he's now a color man for baseball on TV.

THROWING IN THE SPONGE

White Sox catcher Jim Essian was known for stretching the rules, and once he got clean away with a dirty trick. On a double steal, he threw a white sponge, hidden in his mitt, to second base. The runner who had reached third started home. This time Essian threw the *ball*, and the runner was picked off.

"The Best Catcher of All Time" — One

Josh Gibson may have been the best backstop ever, but we'll never know for sure. He wasn't allowed to play in the majors. A Negro League star for 15 years, Gibson was the catcher for Satchel Paige, and a magnificent hitter. One home run was measured at 575 feet (175 m) — and it wasn't his longest. His 17-year batting average was over .350. Hall of Fame pitcher Walter Johnson said of him: "He hits the ball a mile; he catches so easily, he might as well be in a rocking chair; [he] throws like a bullet." Gibson died of a brain hemorrhage at age 35 — just three months before Jackie Robinson broke the color bar. He finally made it into the Hall of Fame 25 years later in 1972, the second black player so honored.

Josh Gibson

"The Best Catcher of All Time" — Two

Lawrence "Yogi" Berra (who had a cartoon character, Yogi Bear, named after him) became the Yankees' catcher in 1949 — and the team won five pennants in a row. In the World Series 14 times (and on the winning side 10 times), he's the only catcher to have called a perfect Series game. He holds the record for fielding, too — 148 games without an error. Thick-limbed, thick-skinned and short, he was a low wall behind the plate, and, with 358 career homers, a power-pack beside it.

Yogiisms

Yogi Berra

Yogi is the most quoted man in baseball. Our language is richer — and stranger — because of him. He often made no sense, but the message was always clear: "A nickel ain't worth a dime anymore"; "Ninety percent of this game is half mental"; "No wonder nobody comes here — it's too crowded"; and "I didn't really say all those things that I said." His most famous line? "It ain't over till it's over."

6TH INNING
WHO'S IN CHARGE?

"I couldn't have done it without my players."
Casey Stengel

THE MANAGER
What He Once Was

When baseball changed from a game for rich gents to a business to make rich gents richer, somebody had to be in charge. The first manager was William "Harry" Wright. Born in England, Harry was a professional cricketer and a jeweler — who fell in love with the baseball diamond. In 1858, aged 23, he joined the New York Knickerbockers as a pitcher and fielder. Ten years later, he organized and managed the first pro team, the Cincinnati Red Stockings. He was also their center fielder, relief pitcher, trainer, travel agent, bat-and-ball minder, cashier, watchdog, and uniform designer. And he doled out fatherly advice to young players: "Eat hearty.... Roast beef rare will aid.... Live regularly, keep good hours, and avoid intoxicating drinks and tobacco."

BEWARE OF MANAGER

For the next 50 years player-managers like Wright were the rule. (Pete Rose, also of Cincinnati, was the last. His playing days were over in 1986 — and his baseball days in 1989, after he was suspended from baseball for life because of gambling). Those early managers invented or perfected many aspects of the game: Chicago's Cap Anson was the first to take his team south for spring training, in 1886; Ned Hanlon of the scrappy trash-talking 1890s Baltimore Orioles made signals, the bunt, and the hit-and-run play part of his everyday strategy.

John McGraw, the runty (5 feet, 7 inches, 150 pounds/ 1.7 m, 68 kg) Baltimore third baseman, took over the New York Giants in 1902. He brought with him the Orioles' strategic weapons, street-gang style, and four-letter words, and became one of the best managers in history. It was he who first tried relief pitchers, pinch-hitters, and defensive shifts — positioning the fielders where the batters were likely to hit the ball. A hot-tempered roughneck who ran on fire in his belly and hate in his heart, McGraw was called "Little Napoleon" because he demanded total obedience. He once fined infielder Sammy Strang, who hit only 16 homers lifetime, $25 (equal to a couple of weeks' pay) for hitting a home run with two men on, when he'd been ordered to bunt. McGraw got into fist-fights with owners, managers, players, umpires, batboys, fans, and complete strangers. He made baseball exciting and unpredictable, and the grandstands were full when he came to town. McGraw led the Giants to a record 10 pennants, and in 33 years he won 2,840 games, second on the all-time win list.

First on the all-time win list, with 3,776 wins, was Connie Mack, manager of the Philadelphia Athletics. (It took him 53 years, the longest any manager has managed to manage — but he owned the team.) He was everything John McGraw wasn't: tall, elegant, and gentlemanly. Mr. Mack never swore, never raised his voice, and never wore a uniform — which meant he couldn't set foot on the field. He directed his troops from the dugout by gesturing with his lineup card, dressed always in a white shirt with a high starched collar, a suit and tie, and a straw hat. It was Connie Mack who said — softly — after losing 117 games in 1917, "You can't win 'em all."

Connie Mack

57

Destined to become one of the greatest managers of all time, Charles Dillon Stengel's first ambition was to be the only left-handed dentist in Kansas City. But drilling a ball turned out to be more fun than drilling a tooth. Called "Casey" after his home town of K.C., Stengel played outfield for 16 years. His finest moments came as a member of John McGraw's New York Giants. In the 1923 World Series, Casey hit two game-winning home runs. (They were the first Series homers hit in Yankee Stadium, and the only games the Giants won.) Stengel's funniest moments came too often to count: once he trapped a sparrow under his cap and when he disagreed with the umpire's call, lifted his cap. The fans were delighted, and so was the sparrow. The umpire wasn't. In one dull spring-training game, Casey dropped out of sight: he hid under a manhole cover, and when a fly ball came his way, his glove popped up like a periscope to make the catch.

As a manager, he got off to a slow start: from 1934 to 1936 his Dodgers stood sixth, fifth, and seventh. In Boston, he managed the Braves to seventh place four times. (His leg was broken when a taxi hit him, and the fans chose the driver as Most Valuable Player.) But in 1949, the Yankees hired him — and he led them to 10 pennants and seven World Series crowns in 12 years. So they fired him.

Two years later, at age 73, he became the first manager of the expansion team, the "Amazin' Mets," who bumbled and bungled their way into the hearts of fans, while Casey moaned, "Can't anybody here play this game?" Casey retired in 1965, and the following year was elected to the Hall of Fame. He died in 1975. The only manager to win five World Series in a row, Casey also won the love of all who loved the game. Clown, showman, a genius on the field (earning him the nickname of "The Ol' Perfessor"), Stengel "played the percentages" — using a left-handed pitcher against a right-handed batter, for example — but he also knew when not to. He had total recall of every game he'd ever managed. Although he once said, "The art of managing is keeping the five guys who hate you away from the five who are undecided," he was admired and loved by his players. He was superb at handling superb men — Joe DiMaggio, Mickey Mantle, Yogi Berra, Eddie Lopat, Whitey Ford, Johnny Sain among them. Casey Stengel gloried in the game, and brought glory to it. As he himself said, "You could look it up."

Huh?

Casey Stengel often bewildered his hearers. Trying to understand him was once described as "picking up quicksilver with boxing gloves." Some samples: "I've always heard it couldn't be done, but sometimes it don't always work" and "The future ain't what it used to be" and "Good pitching will always beat good hitting and vice versa."

Skipper Sketches

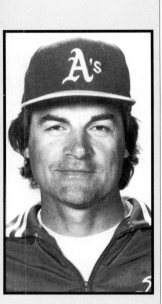

Leo Durocher
Nicknamed "The Lip," Durocher was mouthy, pushy, and sometimes downright nasty. Once, warned early in the game to keep quiet, he pretended to faint with shock when an umpire called one of his players out. The fans laughed; the umpire didn't. He said: "Dead or alive, Durocher, you're out, too." Leo read two books a night, hung out with gangsters, and married a movie star (Laraine Day, who knocked 'em dead in *Dr. Kildare's Strange Case*.) Famous for saying "Nice guys finish last," in 23 years of not being nice, he won 2,010 games, and his 1954 New York Giants won the World Series.

Billy Martin
— the most-fired and most-hired manager in history. Short-fused Yankee owner George Steinbrenner signed him up and kicked him out five times. Martin was a frantic perfectionist who wanted his players to be the same. It paid off: New York won American League pennants in 1976 and 1977, and the World Series in 1977. But Billy was a loser away from the park, drinking and brawling his way into trouble. All trouble ended on Christmas Day, 1989: Billy — who scorned seatbelts — was thrown through the windshield of his pickup truck and broke his neck. He died instantly.

George "Sparky" Anderson
— a terrible player (.218 average in his only year in the majors) but a great manager. (His Cincinnati Reds — "The Big Red Machine" — won five pennants and two World Series in the 1970s, and his 1984 Detroit Tigers were champs, too.) Sparky's goal is to oust his idol, John McGraw, from second place on the managers' win list — and he may well do it. Sparky runs his mouth as fast as he runs his teams: he's a nonstop talker who'll tell you more than you want to know about more than you care about — even if you don't ask. He changes pitchers so often he's called "Captain Hook." but he's good with his players, especially rookies — as long as they don't have hair below, or earrings in, their ears

Tony La Russa
Sometimes accused of "over-managing," Tony La Russa may be the very model of a modern major manager. He controls every aspect of the game, including his own emotions. A lawyer with a poker player's face, La Russa, like Casey Stengel before him, has an awesome memory. He also keeps detailed notes of every pitch and pitcher, every hit and hitter, every play and player, every win, every loss, and everything in between. He must be doing something right: his Oakland As have won three pennants and a World Series.

THE COACHING BOX

Managers and extra players were the first coaches (called "coachers" until about 1915). They directed traffic and sent signs to the runners. They also heckled, yelled X-rated insults, and ran up and down the basepaths to rattle the pitcher. This activity led to them being confined to coaching boxes at first and third in 1887. The rule says that coaches aren't allowed to step out of the boxes, but umpires ignore it unless they stray too far.

The first full-time coach was Arlie Latham, a hard-drinking, fast-living, sleazy little third baseman with a big mouth, hired by John McGraw in 1909. The Giants' fans liked him (he danced jigs in the coaching box), but they didn't introduce him to their sisters.

The first-base coach passes on signals, helps the runner avoid pickoffs, and reminds him of stuff he shouldn't forget but sometimes does: the count (balls and strikes on the batter), the score, the inning, and the number of outs. The third-base coach does much more: he waves the runner on to score, or holds him up (so he must know the arm strength of all opposing players); he relays signs from the dugout to all base-runners and the batter; and he does all this with great speed.

Sometimes he gets a bit too much in the game: Mike Kelly (king of the slide), coaching at third for Boston in a game with Pittsburgh, tricked a rookie pitcher. With the score tied in the bottom of the ninth and a runner on third, Kelly said, "Let's see the ball, son," and the kid lobbed it over. Kelly let it bounce away, and the runner scored.

The first pitching coach, Wilbert Robinson, was also hired by John McGraw, in 1911. "Uncle Robby," a star Orioles' catcher who once got seven hits in seven at-bats, had a knack for helping pitchers. His most famous pupil was Hall of Fame southpaw Rube Marquard. In his first three years, without Robinson, Marquard won nine games; in the next three, under Uncle Robby's patient teaching, he won 73.

Pitching coaches 'visit the mound," presumably to offer advice. Once Bob Gibson, coach for the Braves, trotted out to chat with a hurler who was getting shelled. Then the pitcher settled down and threw strikes. Asked later what he'd said, Gibson answered, "I just told him that if there weren't 15,000 people watching, I'd hit him in the head."

Teams didn't hire batting coaches until around 1950.

Sometimes the best coaches are not the best hitters — renowned coaches Charlie Lau and Walter Hriniak never hit above .255. But sometimes they are: Rod Carew, hitting coach for the California Angels, retired with a career average of .328 and a hit total of 3,053.

"Throw strikes or you pay for the pizza."

THE MANAGER
What He Now Does

The main job of the manager is to win, or rather to worry about winning. He worries about his pitchers and the other team's hitters. He worries about his hitters and the other team's pitchers. He worries about who's hurt and who's shirking, who's hot and who's not, about the shortstop with an attitude and the fielder with fingers of stone. In his spare time, he worries about whether he'll still be manager at the end of the week. (Someone once said that the best qualification for the manager's job is to be independently wealthy.)

But 162 times a year — and more if he's lucky — the manager has a few other jobs to do. He puts on a uniform — the only manager of a pro sport who does so. He makes up the lineup card — setting out which players will bat that day and in what order. He decides when to send in a new pitcher, a pinch-runner, a pinch-hitter, or a pinch-anything. And he calls the plays — bunt, steal, take a pitch, hit and run, run and hit, swing away. And he hopes he's done the right thing. In other words, the manager gets the first guess at what might work. (If it doesn't, there's never a shortage of second-guessers.)

Unlike Harry Wright, the modern manager has an army to help him: batting, pitching, and base coaches; doctors, physiotherapists, trainers, and exercise experts (including, once, a ballerina); psychiatrists, psychologists, "motivators," and other gurus (including, once, a hypnotist for the St. Louis Browns, who then lost 25 games in six weeks — maybe they were playing in a trance); someone to make sure the team travels from A to B without delay or disaster; and someone to make sure the balls and bats and gloves get there before the game starts.

7TH INNING

THE FANS AND THE MEDIA

"Open the window, Aunt Minnie, here it comes!"
Home run call of Pirates play-by-play announcer Rosey Rowswell
(who then would smash a light bulb near the microphone)

FANS ...

The manager may get the first guess, but ready with the second guess is a huge army of fans. Some are manager-wannabes who crowd the grandstands and the phone-in shows, letting the real manager know that, if he had any smarts and/or guts, he would have called for a bunt, yanked the pitcher in the third inning, and used a pinch-hitter for the guy who's 0-for-23. Others are dedicated scholars of the game who know its history, enjoy its complexity — and would have called for a bunt, yanked the pitcher in the third inning, and used a pinch-hitter for the guy who's 0-for-23.

Some experts claim that the word "fan" comes from "the Fancy," English slang for people who loved boxing. (A "fancy-bloke" was a sporting man.) But "fann" was used 400 years ago, shortened from "fanatic" — a person so deranged with enthusiasm he was locked up in the local insane asylum to protect the public. From about 1890 to 1910, a fan was also called a "crank." The ancient Anglo-Saxon word "cranc" means "fallen in battle," and through the centuries it came to mean "sick," or "disordered in the mind." Know any fans like that?

In the early years of baseball, some fans were often rowdy, drunken, violent, and eager to interfere in the game. When Cincinnati played

Brooklyn on June 14, 1870, a fan tackled a Cincinnati outfielder to stop him from making a play, and the Red Stockings' 84-win streak came to an end. Fights in the stands were common. Bottles (empty) rained down on the field, umpires, of course, being the favorite target. Gamblers openly took bets, often from the players. By 1910 or so, the field of dreams sometimes seemed more like a field of battle — or a den of thieves.

Baseball had to clean up its act. It outlawed gambling, a move that was finally successful after the 1919 Black Sox Scandal. It instituted "Ladies' Day" (women were admitted free with a male escort, the theory being that men would behave better and, as Alfred Spink wrote in *The Sporting News*, be "more selective in their choice of adjectives"). It hired ushers — very large ushers, more like bouncers — but only after May 15, 1912, the day Ty Cobb vaulted into the stands and beat up one Claude Lucker, said to be "a helpless cripple" (before Cobb punched him).

The Song helped, too: "Take Me Out to the Ball Game," composed in 1908, was a hit. Soon it was sung at all ballparks, making people believe — again — that baseball was a gentle game, even a noble game. Men, women, and children flocked to the parks.

Fans still get surly once in a while. Pete Rose was the target of rotting vegetables after a hard slide into Mets' shortstop Bud Harrelson in 1973. Twenty years later, in 1993, Angels' fans threw baseballs — more dangerous than moldy tomatoes — at an opposing team. And through the 1970s and 1980s, gangs of no-brainers rampaged through city streets torching cars and looting shops to "celebrate" victories. But by and large, baseball remains a peaceful spectacle.

Some fans do some very strange things: Minnesota fans wave pieces of white cloth, called "homer hankies"; Toronto fans wave — once in a while — big blue sponges in the shape of a "J"; in Atlanta, in spite of protests by some Native Americans, they wave red rubber tomahawks to cheer on the Braves; and everywhere they *do* the wave, standing up, section by section, all around the park (except in Chicago Cubs' Wrigley Field, where purist fans won't even wave goodbye). Fans wave flags and banners and bedsheets and articles of clothing. Sometimes fans remove their clothing, giving a whole new meaning to the term "Bleacher Bums." Fans paint their bodies in team colors. Fans shave their scalps to show the team logo. Fans wear feathers, and beaks, and cones on their heads. Some fans do some very strange things.

AND FANS . . .

But other fans wouldn't be caught dead doing any of the above. While they may cheer their favorite team, they have a higher loyalty — to the game itself. They know the rules; they understand the patterns and rhythms as the game unfolds; they are made happy by the orderly beauty of a game well-played. Often you'll see them at the ballpark, sitting quietly, keeping score perhaps, or nodding in approval at a perfect bunt, a fine double play, a shrewd bit of base-running. These are the fans who enjoy a pitchers' duel that ends in a score of 1-0. These are the fans who love the strategies of the game, the moves and counter-moves, the games-within-a-game between pitcher and batter, catcher and runner, manager and manager. These are the true fans of baseball.

Frisking the Fans

Many parks examine fans' bags and knapsacks at the door. Bottles and cans are banned. In the Dominican Republic, *fanáticos* are frisked by armed guards — for guns and machetes.

CARDS AND COLLECTIBLES

Fans are also collectors. You name it, they collect it — broken bats, bruised baseballs, "game-used" jerseys, gloves, spikes, ticket stubs, sheet music, photos, posters, pennants, caps, autographed anythings, and cards.

Especially cards. It started way back around 1860, with tintypes (photographs on tin), and visiting cards with tiny team photos. In 1886, Old Judge Cigarettes began to give away, with every pack of smokes, a card with a photo of a player faking a cut at a ball on a string. The most famous and most valuable cards date from 1909 to 1911, when the American Tobacco Company printed a set of 524 top stars. (Among them is the rarest card, that of Honus Wagner. Upset that his picture was used to sell tobacco to young people, Wagner made the company stop printing it. Only 12 or so are left, each worth more than $200,000.) Later, candy and gum companies issued cards to attract kids — Cracker Jack, Goudey Gum, U.S. Caramel, Chiclets, Gum, Inc. — and finally Topps in 1950. Cards have come with newspapers, bread, cookies, cereal, ice cream, potato chips, soft drinks, and wieners.

What was once a kid's hobby was taken over by greedy grown-ups in the 1980s. Cards were bought as investments, not out of love for collecting or for the game. Card prices skyrocketed — way out of reach for kids. Now the bubble-gum bubble has burst: a card costing $100 five years ago may now be had for $10. A lot of grown-ups lost a lot of money. Serves them right.

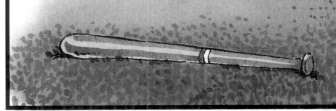

7TH INNING STR

It's the middle of the seventh inning. The home team runs off the field — and all the fans stand up.

Why? How did the "seventh inning stretch" begin? Some think U.S. President William Howard Taft is at the bottom of it, so to speak. At a Pittsburgh Pirates game in 1910, when the presidential backside grew numb, the Chief Exec stood up — and everyone in the park stood, too, as a mark of respect.

But way back in 1869, Harry Wright, famous player-manager of the Cincinnati Red Stockings, wrote to a friend: "The spectators all arise between halves of the seventh inning, extend their legs and arms and sometimes walk about. In so doing they enjoy the relief afforded by relaxation from a long posture upon hard benches."

Since 1908, the fans do more than extend their legs and arms. They sing — and in nearly every ballpark it's the same song. One afternoon, vaudeville actor and lyricist Jack Norworth (real name John Klem) took a New York subway ride. As he stood swaying from a strap he noticed an ad for a baseball game. Jack had never seen a game (and didn't until 1942) but half an hour later he'd written the two verses and chorus of his greatest hit. "Take Me Out to the Ball Game" ranks third on the all-time list of songs sung in the United States — only "Happy Birthday" and "The Stars and Stripes Forever" are belted out more often. (Jack had more wives — five — than hits — two: of his more than 2500 songs, only one other, "Shine On, Harvest Moon," is remembered today.)

Jack's partner Albert von Tilzer wrote the music. Some of his songs are still around — "Alcoholic Blues," "I'll Be With You In Apple

Blossom Time," and "Put Your Arms Around Me, Honey, Hold Me Tight." Mercifully forgotten are "Nora Malone, Call Me by Phone," "Wait Till You Get Them Up in the Air, Boys," and "Oh! How She Could Yacki, Hacki, Wicki, Wacki Woo."

In the first hastily scribbled version, the heroine of the song was Katie Casey, but Jack later changed her name to Nelly Kelly. In case you wonder why everyone remembers only the chorus here's the complete lyric:

ETCH

(Verse 1)

Nelly Kelly loved baseball games,
Knew the players, knew all their
        names,
You could see her there ev'ry day,
Shout "Hurray," when they'd play.
Her boy friend by the name of Joe
Said, "To Coney Isle, dear, let's go,"
Then Nelly started to fret and pout,
And to him I heard her shout.

(Chorus)

Take me out to the ball game,
Take me out with the crowd,
Buy me some peanuts and
        crackerjack,
I don't care if I never get back.
Let me root root root for the home
        team,
If they don't win it's a shame,
For it's one, two, three strikes you're
        out
At the old ball game.

(Verse 2)

Nelly Kelly was sure some fan,
She would root just like any man,
Told the umpire he was wrong,
All along, good and strong.
When the score was just two and
        two,
Nelly Kelly knew what to do,
Just to cheer up the boys she knew,
She made the gang sing this song.

THE MEDIA

The link between the fans and the game is the media — the people who write about baseball and talk about baseball for a living. (They're great second-guessers, too.) And each depends on the other: without the fan, there'd be no need for baseball writers and broadcasters; without the media, there'd be fewer fans. It's a partnership that's good for both partners — and for baseball, too.

Newspapers and Magazines

Henry Chadwick, the only writer so far in the Hall of Fame, was the first great baseball reporter. Born in England in 1834, where he'd played cricket and rounders, Henry came to the United States when he was 13. When he found baseball, he found his life's work. By 1858, he'd already written the game's first rule book. Chadwick also wrote the first guide, *Beadle's Dime Base-Ball Player*, in 1860, and the first hardcover book, *The Game of Base Ball*, in 1868. As a reporter for New York and Brooklyn newspapers, Chadwick invented the box score and pioneered many rule changes as the game grew. When he died in 1908, just after going to Opening Day in Brooklyn, the flags in the major league parks flew at half-mast.

Now it's a rare newspaper that doesn't have a baseball reporter. Some have three or four or more. The best ones — early writers such as Ring Lardner, Hugh Fullerton, Grantland Rice, and Damon Runyon, and today's Roger Angell of *The New Yorker* magazine and Thomas Boswell of the *Washington Post* — have followed Chadwick's example. They know the game, they love the game, and they write about the game with honesty, intelligence, and style.

Life wasn't easy for the early reporters. When telegraph operators sent game reports from the park — to the poolroom across town or the saloon across the country — some team owners tried to prevent it. They were afraid people wouldn't come to the games if they could read about them, and they got really nervous about newspaper reports.

But Alfred H. Spink understood that "baseball sells newspapers and newspapers sell baseball." On March 17, 1886, he published the first issue of *The Sporting News*. It sold for five cents. Alfred's nephew Taylor Spink took it over in 1914, and until the 1940s, the newspaper was devoted entirely to baseball. This week's scoop and last night's scandal, a piece of the past and a peek at the future, the box scores from Omaha

and the best sports writing in the country — you could find them all in *The Sporting News*. The Spinks sold a lot of newspapers — *The Sporting News* is still among the most widely read — and a lot of baseball.

Read All About It

Spink started something big. Today there are hundreds, maybe thousands, of newspapers, newsletters, and magazines about what a dying Babe Ruth called "the only real game in the world." There's one about umpires, and one about fantasy camps; there's one about autographs, one about pins and buttons, and dozens about cards; there's one about women players, one about Japanese players, and one about dead players. There's even one about baseball newspapers, newsletters, and magazines. And if you can't find one you like, start your own. Tyler Kepner of Gwynedd Valley, Pennsylvania, did when he was 14. In 1989, he began to publish *KP Baseball Monthly*, a 24-page newsletter of profiles, articles, contests, trivia, and book reviews, now sent to 40 states. Tyler even has his own baseball card.

So read the sign on many a press box at the ballpark about 50 years ago. Women baseball writers, few as they were, were not welcome. They had to put up with vicious abuse, bad jokes, nasty pranks, and breathtaking stupidity from male reporters and from players. And they couldn't do their job properly because they weren't allowed into players' locker rooms — which often had a "No Dogs or Women" sign on the door.

In 1979 baseball commissioner Bowie Kuhn edged into the 20th century and ruled that female reporters should have the same rights as male. As Alison Gordon, who covered the Toronto Blue Jays for five years and now writes baseball mysteries, said: ". . . opening the clubhouse doors didn't lead to the end of the world or of baseball as we know it." But some players (and managers and owners) didn't get it. Macho hitter Dave Kingman once sent a live rat to a woman writer. Conditions are still far from perfect — and while women have proved they can do the job, few are given the chance.

TYLER KEPNER
KP BASEBALL MONTHLY   1992

A Giant Step Forward

"Ladies and gentlemen, welcome to Candlestick Park," were the first words from Sherry Davis, the first full-time female public address announcer in major league baseball. She began the job on April 12, 1993, at the San Francisco Giants' home opener against Florida.

Radio

On the afternoon of August 5, 1921, people in Pittsburgh fiddled with their crystal set radios and found a miracle: the Phillies and Pirates, playing baseball, at Forbes Field. The first play-by-play was being announced by Harold Arlin of KDKA, a station owned by Westinghouse Electric where Arlin was a foreman. (The Pirates won, 8-5.)

Fans loved the idea, but team owners (except Phil Wrigley, who asked Chicago stations to air Cubs' games in 1925) were wary. If you could listen for nothing, they argued, why buy a ticket?

Wrong again. Radio, like newspapers earlier (and television later), brought baseball more interest, more fans — and more money. The owners cheered up when they figured out they could sell broadcast rights to stations, who in turn sold time to advertisers. Henry Ford, the car-maker, paid $400,000 to sponsor the World Series from 1934 to 1937. By 1939, games of all major league teams were on the radio. When portable radios came along, fans brought them to the ballpark. They still do: baseball and radio were made for each other.

The Great Pretender

For the first 30 years, home-town radio announcers re-created away games from telegraphed play-by-play summaries, with "canned" crowd noise (volume to the max for a home run) and sound effects. The crack of a bat might be made by striking a wooden block with a pencil and a fastball thunking into the catcher's mitt became a popping cork. It was "Let's Pretend," to fool fans who were happy to be fooled. A young man in Des Moines named Ron "Dutch" Reagan was especially good at it. Later he got a job in Washington.

THE VOICES OF SUMMER

Announcers such as Walter (Red) Barber, Vin Scully, Mel Allen, Ernie Harwell, and Harry Caray were soon stars, as well known as Roger Maris, Ted Williams, and Sandy Koufax. Red Barber, born in Mississippi in 1908, the year Henry Chadwick died, set the standard. He landed a job with Cincinnati in 1934, switched to the Dodgers in 1939, and to the Yankees in 1963. He made up — or made popular — the expressions, "in the catbird seat" (in control), "tearin' up the peapatch" (rallying for runs), and "rhubarb" (a fight or general chaos on the field).

With the Southerner's gift for story-telling, he also knew his baseball: he studied the stats and talked for hours with the players before every game. And

Walter (Red) Barber

like all great reporters, he told the truth. It got him fired. In 1966 he announced that there were exactly 413 fans in Yankee Stadium that afternoon. The next day he was outta there. Voted into the Hall of Fame in 1978, he died in October 1992, in the middle of the World Series.

Harry Caray (born Carabina) was orphaned at 10 and grew up in foster homes, poor and not very happy, but with a passion for baseball. He quit school at 16 and sold newspapers, making 43 cents a day. Now he's a millionaire, a cult hero, and in the Hall of Fame. With the Cardinals for 25 years, Harry moved to the Chicago White Sox in 1969, then to the Cubs, where he's still going strong.

Harry's famous — and always forgiven — for on-air goofs, cheering the home team, and butchering "Take Me Out to the Ball Game" during the seventh-inning stretch. He says it's the only song he

Harry Caray

knows the words to. His son Harry II (Skip) and his grandson Harry III (Chip) are also in the booth: they're announcers for the Atlanta Braves.

OOOPS!
An announcer in the minor leagues, perhaps sick of his job, once said: "Syracuse is threatening, and Cubs' [pitcher] Tony Jacobs is throwing up in the bullpen."

TV

On August 26, 1939, a week before World War Two began, about 75 New Yorkers sat in their living-rooms watching and listening to a round glass screen the size of a dinnerplate. They were watching the first televised baseball game in the United States, in glorious black and white (and shades of gray), between the Brooklyn Dodgers and the Cincinnati Reds. They were listening to the comfortable drawl of Red Barber, doing the play-by-play (and the commercials) for the just-born TV station W2XBS.

Some 36 years later, on October 22, 1975, about 75 million North Americans watched the seventh game of the World Series between Boston and Cincinnati. (The Red Sox didn't win, of course: they haven't since they sold Babe Ruth to the Yankees in 1918. They call it "The Curse of the Bambino.") The little glass screen had come a long way.

At first, team owners put up a fight (again), banning telecasts in major league cities. Finally, in the 1970s, when football threatened to gobble up most of the prime time, most of the fans, and most of the cash, the owners struck a deal. The fortune they got for broadcast rights came just in time. The players, under their union chief Marvin Miller, had won the right to be "free agents" after six years' service; that is, they could move to whatever team offered the most money. Which is why Barry Bonds makes $7,291,667 a year.

In the 1980s, cable television and superchannels such as TBS, ESPN, and WGN brought even more games into our homes — and more of us to the ballpark. By the year 2000, there's sure to be a "Baseball Channel," so you can watch games until you go batty. And when the new satellite nicknamed the "Death Star" is parked in outer space, you'll be able to second-guess the manager in any ball game, anywhere, any time — and all you'll need is a metal dish about the size of a dinnerplate.

8TH INNING

BALLPARK FIGURES

"You could look it up."
Casey Stengel

Baseball is a numbers game. Strikeouts and steals, sacrifices and saves, grounders and grand slams, runs batted in and runners left on — baseball creates Niagaras of numbers, and then plays with them. No other sport is so endlessly countable, so teeming with arithmetic.

At the heart of the game is the number three. Three strikes and you're out; three outs and your team's out; you must touch three bases before you come home; a team has three times three players; a game has three times three innings; and a game doesn't end until a pitcher gets three times three times three outs.

Why three? Three is magical, mighty, and mysterious and has been so since humans first put one thing and one thing and one thing together. Three is how we think of time — the past, the present, the future; and how we think of story — the beginning, the middle, the end. Three notes of the scale make a harmonious sound, a chord. Three — a trinity — is in many world religions.

We say, "I'll give you three guesses" and "Good things come in threes." We give three cheers. When we're small, we listen to *The Three Bears, Three Little Kittens, Three Blind Mice*, and *The Three Little Pigs*. When we learn the alphabet, we know our ABCs. Then we read fairy tales, in which a king has three sons or daughters, a genie grants three wishes, and the hero must perform three great deeds.

Three is magical, mighty, and mysterious — just like baseball.

THE UMPIRE STRIKES BACK

Back in the days when there were only three umpires in a game, the song "Three Blind Mice" was banned from all ballparks.

SOME NUMBERS, ODD AND EVEN (BUT MOSTLY ODD), ABOUT BASEBALL

0 Uniform number worn by Al Oliver when he joined the Texas Rangers, after being a Pittsburgh Pirate for nine years. He said he wanted to start fresh.

0.00 The ERA of New York Giants' pitchers in the 1905 World Series, when the Series was the best-of-five (three again!) games.

0 - 0 - 0 A perfect game by a pitcher: no runs, no hits, no walks recorded by opposing team.

1 The number of players who ever pinch-hit for Ted Williams and Carl Yastrzemski — Carroll Hardy, who did it for both of them.

1.75 The lowest ERA for left-handed pitchers in the American League for one season — a record set by Babe Ruth in 1916.

3 The number of shutouts pitched by New York Giants' Christy Mathewson in the 1905 World Series.

3 The number of commercials shown on the first televised baseball game in 1939, one each for Ivory Soap, Mobil Oil, and Wheaties.

3.6 The number of seconds it took Cardinal Enos Slaughter to run from home to first base in the 1946 World Series against Boston. After a teammate singled, he ran from first to home in 10 seconds. His run won the Series — and he was playing with a broken elbow.

5 The largest number of brothers from one family who played in the major leagues. Ed, Tom, Jim, Frank, and Joe Delahanty played during the years 1888 to 1909. With a career batting average of .346 (over .400 three times), Ed's in the Hall of Fame. His death was strange. In 1903, drunk and waving a straight razor, he was put off a train in Canada, across from Buffalo. Walking along the railway bridge over the Niagara River, Ed met a conductor, with whom he had a scuffle. His body was found below Niagara Falls eight days later. No one knew (or told) what really happened.

7 Most U.S. Presidents in power during one baseball career. Nolan Ryan pitched under Johnson, Nixon, Ford, Carter, Reagan, Bush, and Clinton.

9 The number of Dominican-born shortstops playing in major league games on one day in April 1986. Four were from San Pedro de Macoris, "The Shortstop Factory."

10 The dollars charged for a Boston season ticket in the 1880s — if it was for a woman. Men had to pay $15.

12 The number of intentional walks to Yankee Babe Ruth in the 1926 World Series against the Cardinals. Ruth got angry after the twelfth walk (in the ninth inning of the seventh game with two out, and the Cards leading 3-2), tried to steal second base and was thrown out. The Cards won the Series. It's been called the only stupid play of Ruth's career.

13 The number of years between hits for knuckleball pitcher Charlie Hough. On June 4, 1980, he hit safely for the Dodgers. Then he moved to the American League, where pitchers don't hit. In 1993 he joined the NL expansion team, the Florida Marlins, and on June 4, 1993, hit a single off San Diego pitcher Tim Scott.

15 Age of the youngest player to appear in a major league game. Joe Nuxhall, a 6 foot, 3 inch, 195-pound (1.9 m, 88.5 kg) lefty, pitched one inning for Cincinnati in 1944. (With so many players gone to war, teams signed up anyone they could find.) He gave up two hits and five walks. Joe came back to the Reds in 1952, at the more respectable age of 22, and pitched well for the next 15 seasons.

17 Fewest fans ever to watch a game, in Pittsburgh in 1890 — and only six of them bought tickets.

22 The most batters faced by a pitcher in one inning. On June 18, 1894, Baltimore pitcher Anthony Mullane couldn't get anybody out. Sixteen runs were scored — in the first inning.

25 The number of innings played in the longest game. The game began on May 8, 1984, and was stopped at 1.05 a.m. on May 9, after 17 innings. It continued later that day, until the White Sox beat the Brewers 7-6. Finally.

35 The most runs allowed by a pitcher in one game — by Cleveland's David Rowe, on July 24, 1882.

46 In 1993, the average salary of a major-league baseball player was 46 times the average salary of an ordinary worker.

82 The height in inches (6 feet, 10 inch/ 2.08 m) of baseball's tallest player, pitcher Randy Johnson. His hair is tall, too.

116 Most games won in a season — by Chicago Cubs, in 1906.

134 Most games lost in a season — by Cleveland, in 1899.

154 The number of seagulls eating bugs in center field in Milwaukee's County Stadium, June 12, 1993, as the Brewers and Yankees tried to play a baseball game. Gus the Wonder Dog, a yellow Labrador retriever, finally chased the birds away.

267 The record number of times a major league player has been hit by a pitched ball — held by Don "Bruise" Baylor in a 19-year career.

296 The number of feet (90 m) Mildred "Babe" Zaharias, All-American and Olympic athlete, threw a baseball on July 25, 1931, at Jersey City. A champion in running, jumping, hurdling, basketball, football, swimming, golf, and baseball, Babe played outfield with a barnstorming team and could hit the plate from deep center. Canadian Edward Gorbous holds the record for the longest throw: on August 1, 1957, he tossed a ball 445 feet, 10 inches (135.8 m).

440 The number of dollars paid at an auction for a toothpick found in ace pitcher Tom Seaver's uniform jacket; bought by the same mad fan who bought a piece of Joe DiMaggio's wedding cake (from his first marriage).

573 The number of feet (175 m) in the longest measured major league home run, by Dave Nicholson of the White Sox on May 6, 1964.

1,066 The number of bases stolen by Rickey Henderson by June 16, 1993, to make him the all-time leader on the planet. He surpassed the record of 1,065, held by Yutaka Fukumoto of the Japanese League. Yutaka gave Rickey a pair of gold shoes to mark the event.

2,500 The number of dollars Angels' pitcher Julio Valera got each month in 1993 if his body fat was lower than the month before.

13,162 The number of players in the major leagues from 1871 to 1993.

93,103 The highest number of fans at a baseball game — on May 7, 1959, when the Los Angeles Dodgers honored their catcher Roy Campanella after he was paralyzed in a car accident.

1,000,000 The millionth run in major league history was scored by Houston's Bob Watson on May 4, 1975, against San Francisco at Candlestick Park.

173,000,000 The number of dollars it took to buy the Baltimore Orioles in 1993, the highest amount ever for a major-league team.

What's the Score?

Here's what the earliest surviving scorecard, dated October 17, 1845, looked like:

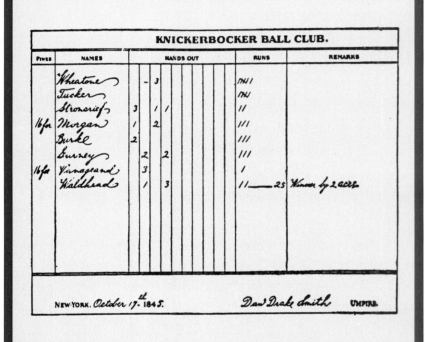

It tells us the game was over after the fourth inning, with the Knickerbockers winning by two "aces." It tells us that only eight players showed up for the game — and that two of them were fined for swearing. There's no way to tell when the runs were scored, and no mention of who pitched.

Back then, games ended as soon as one of the teams scored 21 "aces" (runs). This didn't work very well. Sometimes a game took 20 minutes: sometimes it took five hours. If Team A got 21 "aces" in one or two innings, Team B didn't get a chance to catch up. So in 1857, "Doc" Adams changed the rule: the game became nine innings.

Soon after that Henry Chadwick invented the box score. Packed with facts, weighty with numbers, the box score contains within its tidy borders hours of complicated action. Triumph, defeat, excitement, and suspense are in there, too, often with a touch of revenge or goofiness — if you know how to read it.

HOW TO READ A BOX SCORE

So how did your team do last night? Get the newspaper off the porch, and turn to the sports pages. There's the whole game in five square inches.

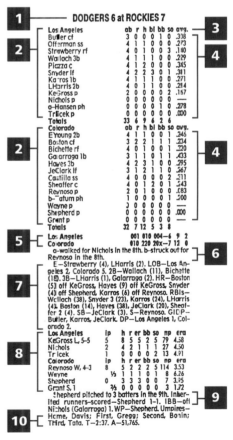

1. Who played, where they played, and who won: the Colorado Rockies beat the LA Dodgers 7-6, at the Rockies' home park in Mile-High Stadium.

2. The batting order (lineup) and positions of each player: so Darryl Strawberry batted third and played right field (rf) for the Dodgers; Vinny Castilla batted seventh and played shortstop (ss) for the Rockies; Jim Tatum came into the game in the eighth inning as a pinch-hitter (ph) for pitcher (p) Armando Reynoso, batting ninth.

3. How the players did at the plate. Cory Snyder had a fab game: in four at-bats (ab), he scored two runs (r) on two hits (h), drove in three runs (bi = batted in). He didn't draw a walk (bb = base on balls), and struck out (so) only once.

4. The batting averages for each player for the season so far. Now you see why the manager put in a pinch-hitter for Reynoso: his average is .083. A batting average is the number of hits a batter would get if he had a thousand at-bats, based on his record. Armando would get 83. Not terrific. Averages over .300, like Snyder's, *are* terrific. Andres Galarraga's .433 blows your mind.

5. The line score, showing which inning the runs were scored in, and the total runs, hits, and errors for each team. The "x" in the bottom of the ninth inning means it didn't have to be played because Colorado had already won. (The home team always bats in the bottom of the inning).

6. Who the pinch-hitters replaced, when they came into the game, and what they did at the plate.

7. The details of defense, hitting, and base-running. The numbers in parentheses are the season totals to date. E = error; LOB = runners left on base at the ends of innings; 2B, 3B, and HR = double, triple, and home run; RBIs = runs batted in; SB = stolen base; S = sacrifice bunt; GIDP = grounded into double play; and DP = double plays by each team. (Other plays, which didn't happen in this game, are SF = sacrifice fly; and CS = caught stealing.)

8. The pitching record: who won (W), who lost (L), and their Win/Loss record so far; ip = innings pitched; h = hits given up; r = runs given up; er = earned runs (those that score without the help of errors); bb = bases on balls (walks) issued; so = strike-outs; np = number of pitches; and era = earned run average so far. The earned run average is the number of earned runs a pitcher gives up for every nine innings pitched. (You calculate ERA by multiplying earned runs by 9, then dividing by total innings pitched. For this one game, Reynoso's ERA would be $2 \times 9 = 18$, divided by $8 = 2.25$. An ERA under 3 is good pitching.) Mark Grant got his first save (S) by getting two batters out on three pitches. He "saved" the lead for the winning pitcher.

9. More info about the pitching. When Shepherd began to pitch, three men were on base. One of them scored — which is why the manager got Grant in a hurry. IBB = intentional walk; WP = wild pitch.

10. The umpires' names and their positions; the time (T) it took to play the game, in hours and minutes; and the attendance (A) — nearly 52,000 fans saw the game you just read about.

The only thing you don't know is how the hot dogs tasted.

PRESS CLIPPING

A hundred years ago, when Cornelius McGillicuddy was the catcher for the Pittsburgh Pirates, a typesetter couldn't fit his name into the box score, so he changed it. In the next morning's paper McGillicuddy had become Connie Mack. The name stuck.

They Keep On Running, Running, Running....

In 1870, Cleveland's Forest City team beat the Brooklyn Atlantics 132-1. The game lasted only five innings, maybe because the Cleveland players wore themselves out.

THE OFFICIAL SCORER

The batter hits the ball and runs. The third baseman scoops up the ball and fires it five feet (1.5 m) over the first baseman's head. The batter is safe on first. Does he get a hit? No: the third baseman gets an error. Who says so? The official scorer, that's who.

At every game in the major leagues, an official scorer — usually a retired sports reporter or other knowledgeable person (including, once, a team owner's wife) — judges the play. The official scorer decides base hits, at-bats, stolen bases, wild pitches, passed balls, earned and unearned runs, and just about everything else that happens during the game. The scorer then sends the complete record to the league office within 36 hours. There it becomes a piece of baseball history.

Most scorers' judgments are about errors — plays that with "ordinary effort" could have been made, but weren't. Scorers' decisions can't affect which team wins or loses, but they can end a hit streak, declare a no-hitter, change a pitcher's earned run average, and make a player feel like an idiot.

KEEPING SCORE

Each time a batter steps up to the plate, something happens. The scorecard tells us what, when, and where it happens, who makes it happen, and sometimes, even why. (It doesn't tell us who swore, spit, or argued the call.)

Keeping score is easy after you've done it a few times. (You can buy a scorecard at the game or a sports store. You can even make your own, which is cheaper.)

Here's a simple way to score a game. Each position has a number: the pitcher is 1, the catcher is 2, and so on. (Henry Chadwick — no surprise — devised this system.) Write down on your scorecard the names and position numbers of the players in the lineup. Then, using the symbols shown, mark the progress of the game from the first pitch to the last out. (You can make up your own symbols if you like — as long as you can figure them out when the game's over.)

Symbols

—	Single
=	Double
≡	Triple
≣	Home Run
E	Error
F	Fly
FF	Foul Fly
DP	Double Play
FC	Fielder's Choice
FO	Force Out
HP	Hit by Pitcher
WP	Wild Pitch
BK	Balk
PB	Passed Ball
SB	Stolen Base
CS	Caught Stealing
S	Sacrifice (Bunt)
SF	Sacrifice Fly
KS	Struck Out (swinging)
KC	Struck Out (looking) ("C" = called; umpire calls batter out)
BB	Base on Balls
IBB	Intentional Walk
◯	Player scores

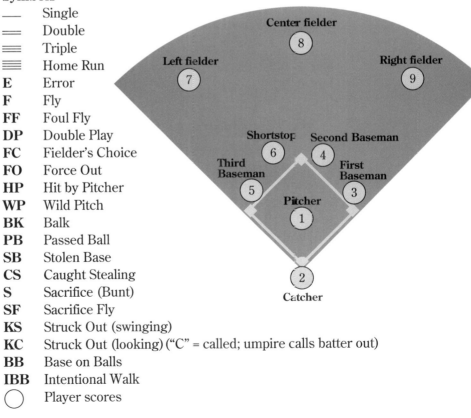

BATTING ORDER	CROSSTOWN CATBIRDS	POSITION NUMBER	INNING 1	2	3	4	5	6	7	8	9	
1	CENTER FIELDER "HIGHPOCKETS"	8	SB ④ BB									
2	SECOND BASEMAN "RABBIT"	4	9 ③ —									
3	DESIGNATED HITTER "HOTSHOT"	DH	F7									
4	RIGHT FIELDER "LASER"	9	3 =									
5	FIRST BASEMAN "LONG JOHN"	3	SF8									
6	SHORTSTOP "TOOTHPICK"	6	KS									
7	THIRD BASEMAN "BEETLES"	5		CS 2-4 HP								
8	CATCHER "CHEW"	2		6-4 —								
9	LEFT FIELDER ""E.T."	7		DP 4-3								
	PITCHER "KNUCKLES"	1										
	TOTALS R/H		2 / 2	0 / 1								

- The lower right is first base,
- upper right is second base,
- upper left is third base, and
- lower left is home plate — so you can see the runners' progress around the bases.

Here's how the Crosstown Catbirds did in their first two innings:

Inning 1

- Highpockets walks, steals second, and scores on Rabbit's single.
- Rabbit singles, advances to third on Laser's double, and scores on Long John's sacrifice fly.
- Hotshot flies out to left field.
- Laser doubles, and advances to third on Long John's sacrifice fly.
- Long John hits a sacrifice fly to center field.
- Toothpick strikes out swinging to end the inning.

Runs = 2; Hits = 2.

Inning 2

- Beetles is hit by a pitch, is awarded first base, and then is caught stealing, on a throw from catcher to second baseman.
- Chew singles, then is out at second, on a throw from shortstop to second baseman (first half of double play).
- E.T. hits into a double play, shortstop to second baseman to first baseman, to end the inning.

Runs = 0; Hits = 1.

On most scorecards there's a place to keep track of how the pitcher did, too: innings pitched (IP), hits (H), runs (R), earned runs (ER), walks (BB), and strikeouts (SO). And usually — but not always — you keep score for both teams.

9TH INNING

MANY WORLDS, MANY WORDS

DISTANT DIAMONDS

"Baseball takes its mystic nine and scatters them wide," a writer once said. He's right. Baseball travels well: it's got legs. Amateur baseball is booming in more than 75 countries, including Sri Lanka, Zimbabwe, the Netherlands Antilles, and Russia, where young men are now learning to swing the *beetah*, hit the *miuch*, and steal second *bahsah*. Cuba — birthplace of U.S. stars Tony Perez, Luis Tiant, and Minnie Minoso — has the best amateur team: they've won more than a dozen world championships, and they took the gold at the 1992 Olympics (the first Games in which baseball was an official sport) without breaking a sweat. Professional ball is a different matter: outside of the United States and Canada, only a handful of countries — the most important being Mexico, Puerto Rico, the Dominican Republic, Venezuela, South Korea, and Japan — have reached pro levels.

"The only real game in the world ... is baseball."
Babe Ruth, at Yankee Stadium, just before he died in 1948

Beisu Bōru

In the 1870s, American missionaries landed in Japan with a Bible in one hand and a baseball in the other. *Beisu bōru* was an immediate hit and was soon in full swing. In 1908 a touring U.S. college team had trouble beating the Japanese six games out of ten, and by the 1920s Japan was ready to turn pro. The country now has two major leagues with six teams apiece. Teams often sign up large North Americans (*gaijin*, "outside people") for home-run power, Cecil Fielder among them. Cecil, nicknamed "The Big Fan" for his many strikeouts, hit two homers right out of the Hanshin Tigers' stadium.

Sadaharu Oh

Games in Japan are very polite: few "brushback" pitches (except to *gaijin*) and much bowing. They last four hours or 12 innings, whichever comes first; and a tie score makes everybody happy. (Except the fans — who scream, swear, throw lighted cigarettes, pound drums, play trumpets, and pack the parks for every game and every batting practice.) Japan is now looking to the Caribbean for young players, with an eye to improving already excellent teams. One day we may see a World Series between the Hiroshima Carp and the Florida Marlins. Go, fish!

OH-OH

Oh means "king" in Japan — and Oh *is* king in Japan. That's Sadaharu Oh — *aikido* master, super swordsman, classy piano player, and all-time home-run king, with 868 dingers in the record books. (He also won 13 RBI titles, nine Gold Gloves, two Triple Crowns, and nine MVP awards.) Oh had an odd batting stance, described as "the crane": he lifted his front leg and balanced on his back leg until he swung. He could do this for up to three minutes without moving. His bats were handmade from a rare tree in northern Japan (and he insisted that only the branches of the female tree be used).

The Spycatcher

In 1934 an All-Star team toured Japan. Among its members were Babe Ruth, Lou Gehrig, Jimmy Foxx — and Moe Berg, a White Sox catcher. Berg, a lawyer who spoke 12 languages, including Japanese, had three baths a day, always wore black, and often disappeared. Which is what he did on November 29, the day of the All-Star game

Wearing a kimono (black), he filmed downtown Tokyo from a hospital roof. Seven years later, when the U.S. got into World War Two, their bombers used Berg's film to pick out targets. Berg quit baseball in 1942 to spy full time, doing wildly dangerous stuff in Nazi Europe. He died in 1972 with a batting average of .243 and a spying average of 1.000. This catcher was never caught looking.

Béisbol

In June 1866, an American freighter docked in Cuba to take on a cargo of sugar. The crew asked the Cuban longshoremen if they'd like to play a game with a bat and a ball. More fun than loading sugar, the Cubans thought, and said *sí*. The rest is history: *béisbol* flowed over the Caribbean like a tidal wave. From the halls of Montezuma to the island canefields to the slopes of the Andes, the game has captured the hearts and minds of boys and young men. For them *béisbol* isn't just a game — it's a passion, a way of life, almost a religion. (It's also, for many, the only way out of grinding poverty.)

Professional teams have flourished in Latin America since the early 1900s. Negro League greats such as Josh Gibson and Ray Dandridge signed up eagerly, sometimes for the money, but often to escape the racism at home. (One black player wrote to an American reporter: "Here, in Mexico, I am a man.") Soon white players traveled south to hone their skills in winter ball. And after Jackie Robinson broke the color bar, Latin players began to travel north. Many became major league stars: Luis Aparicio of Venezuela, Roberto Clemente of Puerto Rico, Dennis Martinez of Nicaragua, Fernando Valenzuela of Mexico, Juan Marichal and the Alous (Felipe, Matty, Jesus and, lately, Moises) of the Dominican Republic, a country that turns out ballplayers the way McDonald's makes hamburgers.

GLIDE, KELLY, GLIDE?

In Canada's Northwest Territories, Inuit kids play baseball under the midnight sun, sometimes on skates.

Words To Know When You Watch:

Béisbol

Lanzador
Pitcher

Jonrón
Home run

Bateador
Batter

Receptor
Catcher

Ponche
Strikeout

Torpedero
Shortstop

Elevado sacrificio
Sacrifice fly

Lanzamiento salvaje
Wild pitch

Doble jugada
Double play

Base robada
Stolen base

Le Baseball

Lanceur
Pitcher

Chandelle
Pop-up

Frappeur
Batter

Receveur
Catcher

Risque-tout
Squeeze play

But volé
Stolen base

Double retrait
Double play

Ballon
Fly ball

Balle papillon
Knuckleball

Coup de circuit
Home run

Beisu Bōru

Picchā
Pitcher

Battā
Batter

Kyattchā
Catcher

Suraidā
Slider

Fōkubōru
Forkball

Sukuizu
Squeeze Play

Banto
Bunt

Waindoappu
Wind-up

Sutoraiku
Strike

Sayonara hōmuran
Game-ending home run

WORDS, WORDS, WORDS...

If baseball is a waterfall of numbers, it's no less a fountain of language. The game gushes with words — funny, sad, made-up, zany, lively words, words that make pictures and words that make poetry. A bat is not just a bat: it's a stick, a chopstick, a banana stick, a baton, a hammer, a pole, a war club, a log, a wand, a toothpick, and a weapon. Nor is a ball just a ball: it's an aspirin, a seed, an apple, a canteloupe, a tomato, an agate, and a pea. And if a hammer hits an apple, it may crush, golf, juice, jack, launch, loft, crank, spank, sting, bash, lash, or smash it, thereby turning it into a bullet, a bug-on-a-rug, a gopher hunter, a seeing-eye single, a dying quail, a can of corn, or a humpback.

Everybody talks baseball, sometimes without knowing it. Baseball has made a hook slide into everyday language. Here are some words and phrases you'll recognize right off the bat: It's a whole new ball game. Keep your eye on the ball. Are you going to play ball? He plays hardball. Stop grandstanding! Give me a rain check. You're way off base! She threw me a curve. I'm batting a thousand. We'll touch base later. That's out of my league. He's in there pitching. Will you go to bat for me? She came through in the clutch. I couldn't get to first base with him. She's got two strikes against her. He gave me a play-by-play of the movie. I call 'em as I see 'em. You're a major league jerk.

Ace threw his heater and Long John golfed a can of corn into right.

And here are a few you might not connect with baseball:

ace — the best pitcher on staff. "Ace" may have meant "best" since the Middle Ages, but it's stayed in fashion because of Asa Brainerd of the 1869 Red Stockings, who pitched every game that season and won 50 out of 57. After that, any pitcher who had a string of wins was called an "asa," which was shortened to "ace." (The "ace" being the most valuable card in some card games helped, too.)

charley horse — a muscle strain or cramp, usually in the legs. First seen in an 1887 newspaper report about a ball game, this term has made it to medical school. There are several versions of its origin, but they all star a horse named Charley. In one version, a bunch of Chicago Cubs went to the racetrack and bet on Charley, a sure winner. In the final stretch, he suddenly went lame and finished last. Thereafter, any player who pulled a leg muscle was called a "Charley horse," and soon it described the injury itself.

hit-and-run — automobile accident in which the driver doesn't stick around; a strategy of striking workers; and anything (or anybody) that attacks swiftly and disappears. It comes directly from the plays devised in the 1890s by Baltimore's Wee Willie Keeler and John McGraw.

jinx — bad luck; something or somebody causing bad luck; to put a hex or a curse on something or somebody. Without baseball, this word might not be with us. The great pitcher Christy Mathewson used it in 1912 in his book *Pitching in a Pinch*. Ballplayers and sports writers picked it up, and soon everybody else did, too. It comes from "jynx," the name of two species of woodpecker in Europe and Africa. Centuries ago, a jynx was thought to have magical powers — it often perched nearby when witches and fortune-tellers brewed their potions and cast their spells. Maybe it still does.

southpaw — this word began life meaning a left-handed pitcher, but now it means any left-handed person. It popped up first in an 1885 newspaper report of a ball game. Back then most ballparks were built with home plate to the west, so the sun wouldn't get in the batters' eyes. (Games were always played in late afternoon.) A left-handed pitcher, facing west, would throw with his southern arm, his "southpaw."

BASEBALL GOES

In 1899, Thomas Edison made a movie called — what else? — *Casey at the Bat*. Since then there have been hundreds of baseball movies (ten called *Casey at the Bat*), but most of them are pretty bad. Do not rush to the video store to squander your allowance on *The Babe*, starring the husband of Roseanne; or *Stealing Home*, in which Jodie Foster dies, probably of embarrassment; or the two sequels to *The Bad News Bears*, which are more bad news than anyone can bear. Save your money for *The Jackie Robinson Story*, starring Jackie himself; the original *The Bad News Bears*, starring Tatum O'Neal as a girl pitcher; *Rookie of the Year* (1973), where Jodie Foster doesn't die, she wins a place on her brother's Little League team; and *The Bingo Long Traveling All-Stars and Motor Kings*, a comedy-adventure about a black barnstorming team of the 1930s.

And then get the whole family to watch *A League of Their Own,* because this is the only way you'll see women play professional baseball. While women and girls have always played baseball — the first organized teams date back to the 1860s — they've never broken into big-league (or Little League until 1974) play. (Does this sound familiar?) But in 1943, with so many male ballplayers gone to war, chewing gum tycoon P.K. Wrigley started the All-American Girls Professional Baseball League. Soon talented women in cutesy skirts played on teams with cutesy names: the Rockford Peaches, the Fort Wayne Daisies, the Milwaukee Chicks, and the Muskegon Lassies. But there was nothing cutesy about their baseball. The played hard — they probably gave 110%.

TO THE MOVIES

Many players came from Canada. The league's first batting champ, with a .322 average, was Gladys Davis of Toronto. Helen Callaghan and her sister Marge hailed from Vancouver. Helen stole 114 bases one season, was dubbed "the female Ted Williams," and won the 1945 batting crown. She taught her son, Casey Candaele of the Astros, how to play ball. (He's not as good as his mother was, maybe because she used a heavier bat.) Helen died in 1992, but not before she and the rest of these remarkable women were honored at Cooperstown.

And you know what? Not one of them threw like a girl.

The New Kid

Mike Makley

Our baseball team never did very much,
we had me and PeeWee and Earl and Dutch.
And the Oak Street Tigers always got beat
until the new kid moved in on our street.

The kid moved in with a mitt and a bat
and an official New York Yankee hat.
The new kid plays shortstop or second base
and can outrun us all in any place.

The kid never muffs a grounder or fly
no matter how hard it's hit or how high.
And the new kid always acts quite polite,
never yelling or spitting or starting a fight.

We were playing the league champs just last week:
they were trying to break our winning streak.
In the last inning the score was one-one,
when the new kid swung and hit a home run.

A few of the kids and their parents say
they don't believe that the new kid should play.
But she's good as me, Dutch, PeeWee, or Earl,
so we don't care that the new kid's a girl.

FAMOUS WORDS ABOUT BASEBALL

Who's on First?

Recognize that question? You should: it's the title of a baseball classic performed by Bud Abbott and Lou Costello, a comedy team of the 1940s. (They made it famous but they didn't make it up: in one guise or another, the routine had been popular in vaudeville for years.) The laughs depend on misunderstandings and mounting confusion. Here's part of it:

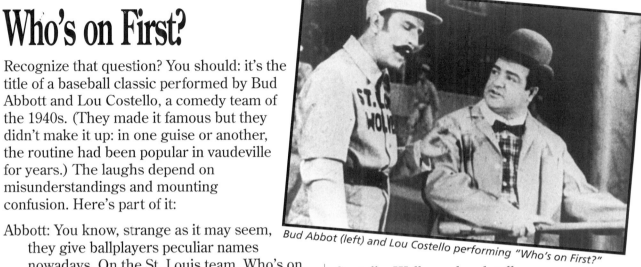

Bud Abbot (left) and Lou Costello performing "Who's on First?"

Abbott: You know, strange as it may seem, they give ballplayers peculiar names nowadays. On the St. Louis team, Who's on first, What's on second, I Don't Know's on third.

Costello: That's what I want to find out. I want you to tell me the names of the fellows on the St. Louis team.

Abbott: I'm telling you. Who's on first, What's on second, I Don't Know's on third.

Costello: You know the fellows' names?

Abbott: Yes.

Costello: Well, then, who's playin' first?

Abbott: Yes.

Costello: I mean the fellow's name on first base.

Abbott: Who.

Costello: The guy on first base.

Abbott: Who is on first base.

Costello: Well, what are you askin' me for?

Abbott: I'm not asking you, I'm telling you. Who is on first base.

Costello: I'm askin' you, who is on first?

Abbott: That's the man's name.

Costello: That's whose name?

Abbott: Yes.

Costello: Well, go ahead, tell me.

Abbott: Who.

Costello: The guy on first.

Abbott: Who.

Costello: The first baseman.

Abbott: Who is on first.

Costello: Have you got a first baseman on first?

Abbott: Certainly.

Costello: Well, all I'm tryin' to find out is what's the guy's name on first base!

Abbott: Oh, no, no. What is on *second base*.

And so it goes, with Costello growing more and more befuddled as they go through the rest of the lineup: the pitcher Tomorrow, the catcher Today, the shortstop I Don't Give A Darn, and fielders Why and Because. (Curious fact: there is no rightfielder. He may have forgotten his name and wandered off the field.) Abbott and Costello performed the sketch thousands of times — on stage, radio, and television. A film of it has a place of honor at the Hall of Fame in Cooperstown.

The Most Famous Words about Baseball

Ernest L. Thayer loved baseball. A brilliant student at Harvard, he edited *The Harvard Lampoon* (a humor magazine), wrote the annual play, and never missed a college ballgame. He graduated in 1885 and hung out in Paris for a while. Then college buddy William Randolph Hearst, who owned the *San Francisco Examiner*, asked Ernest if he'd write some funny pieces for the paper. Ernest said okay, came home, and for the next three years wrote a humor column, often in verse, under the name "Phin." His final column, printed on Sunday, June 8, 1888, was entitled "Casey at the Bat: A Ballad of the Republic, Sung in the Year 1888."

Nobody noticed. But a few months later, vaudeville comedian and singer William DeWolf Hopper, performing at a Broadway theater, wondered aloud to a friend how he might entertain the evening's special guests, the New York Giants and the Chicago White Sox. The friend pulled from his wallet a well-worn newspaper clipping. Hopper recited *Casey at the Bat* that night and the crowd went wild. In five minutes and 40 seconds, Hopper had made himself famous — and made *Casey* immortal.

During the next 45 years, Hopper recited it 10,000 times, and made a good living doing so. But what of "Phin"? Nobody knew who he was. Dozens of impostors claimed authorship, and newspapers and magazines printed the poem whenever — and however badly — they pleased. Only after his friends insisted did Ernest Thayer admit he'd written what was to become the most celebrated poem in the United States. He'd never thought *Casey* was much good, and he was appalled and bewildered by the fuss. He once wrote: "Its persistent vogue is simply unaccountable, and it would be hard to say...if it has given me more pleasure than annoyance."

Casey at the Bat

A Ballad of the Republic, Sung in the Year 1888

The outlook wasn't brilliant for the Mudville nine that day;
The score stood four to two with but one inning more to play.
And then when Cooney died at first, and Barrows did the same,
A sickly silence fell upon the patrons of the game.

A straggling few got up to go in deep despair. The rest
Clung to that hope which springs eternal in the human breast;
They thought if only Casey could but get a whack at that —
We'd put up even money now with Casey at the bat.

But Flynn preceded Casey, as did also Jimmy Blake,
And the former was a lulu and the latter was a cake;
So upon that stricken multitude grim melancholy sat,
For there seemed but little chance of Casey's getting to the bat.

But Flynn let drive a single, to the wonderment of all,
And Blake, the much despis-ed, tore the cover off the ball;
And when the dust had lifted, and men saw what had occurred,
There was Johnnie safe at second and Flynn a-hugging third.

Then from 5000 throats and more there rose a lusty yell;
It rumbled through the valley, it rattled in the dell;
It knocked upon the mountain and recoiled upon the flat,
For Casey, mighty Casey, was advancing to the bat.

There was ease in Casey's manner as he stepped into his place;
There was pride in Casey's bearing and a smile on Casey's face.
And when, responding to the cheers, he lightly doffed his hat,
No stranger in the crowd could doubt 'twas Casey at the bat.

Ten thousand eyes were on him as he rubbed his hands with dirt;
Five thousand tongues applauded when he wiped them on his shirt.
Then while the writhing pitcher ground the ball into his hip,
Defiance gleamed in Casey's eye, a sneer curled Casey's lip.

And now the leather-covered sphere came hurtling through the air,
And Casey stood a-watching it in haughty grandeur there.
Close by the sturdy batsman the ball unheeded sped —
"That ain't my style," said Casey. "Strike one," the umpire said.

From the benches, black with people, there went up a muffled roar,
Like the beating of the storm-waves on a stern and distant shore.
"Kill him! Kill the umpire!" shouted someone on the stand;
And it's likely they'd have killed him had not Casey raised his hand.

With a smile of Christian charity great Casey's visage shone;
He stilled the rising tumult; he bade the game go on;
He signaled to the pitcher, and once more the spheroid flew;
But Casey still ignored it, and the umpire said, "Strike two."

"Fraud!" cried the maddened thousands, and echo answered fraud;
But one scornful look from Casey and the audience was awed.
They saw his face grow stern and cold, they saw his muscles strain,
And they knew that Casey wouldn't let that ball go by again.

The sneer is gone from Casey's lip, his teeth are clenched in hate;
He pounds with cruel violence his bat upon the plate.
And now the pitcher holds the ball, and now he lets it go,
And now the air is shattered by the force of Casey's blow.

Oh, somewhere in this favored land the sun is shining bright;
The band is playing somewhere, and somewhere hearts are light,
And somewhere men are laughing, and somewhere children shout;
But there is no joy in Mudville — mighty Casey has struck out.

Was there a real Casey? No, though many players claimed to be. Was there a real Mudville? No, though many towns claimed to be. And yet both are real. Mudville is the home town of everybody's memory, the scene of our worst nightmares and our best dreams. Mudville is where we were kids, and where it's always summer. Casey — who stands there on the grass under the sun with the crowd cheering his name, who burns with pride and hope and the desire to do a mighty thing, and who then strikes out, fails, in front of 5,000 people — is you, and me, and all of us. And, in spite of the strikeout, there *is* joy in Mudville (and Miami, and Montreal, and Moscow, and Manila, and Melbourne). Where there's a baseball game, there will always be joy.

Glossary

at-bat — to be at home plate in order to hit; an official turn at the plate. If the batter walks, sacrifices, or is hit by a pitch, or is at the plate when a runner is picked off for the third out of an inning, it doesn't count in the statistics as an official "at-bat" (AB).

average — usually, **batting average** (BA), the number of hits a player gets divided by the number of at-bats, taken to three decimal places. Other important averages are **on-base average** (number of times a player reaches base divided by at-bats); **slugging average**, which measures skill at extra-base hits (number of bases safely reached divided by at-bats); and, for pitchers, **earned run average**. See **ERA**.

backstop — the screen behind home plate to protect fans; also, the catcher.

balk — an illegal motion by a pitcher while one or more runners are on base. The Official Rules give 13 types, including dropping the ball, and faking a throw to an empty base. The commonest "balk" occurs when the pitcher doesn't come to the required stop between windup (or stretch) and throw. The penalty? All runners advance one base.

batting order — the list of the nine batters who will begin a game, in the order they come to the plate; also called the **lineup**. It's given to the umpire before the game starts. If you bat out of order, you're automatically out.

bleachers — cheap seats beyond the outfield wall. Originally, a roofless section of unreserved benches without backs, where fans were "bleached" by the sun.

bullpen — where the relief pitchers sit, or get ready to pitch, during a game; also, the group of relief pitchers. The first baseball bullpen was at the Polo Grounds, the home park of the New York Giants, in 1905; but the word had long been used as a holding place for cattle — or prisoners.

designated hitter — a player who doesn't play a position but bats for the pitcher in the American League, a rule adopted in 1973; also called "DH." The first DH was Yankee Ron "Boomer" Blomberg, who ended the 1973 season with a .329 batting average.

double play — two runners are put out in one uninterrupted play.

ERA — earned run average, the most important statistic for a pitcher. It's the average number of runs a pitcher allows for every nine innings pitched, not counting runs scored because of errors. You figure it out by dividing runs scored by innings pitched, then multiplying by nine. It's usually taken to two decimal places.

error — a mistake by the fielding team — such as a dropped ball or a wide throw — that helps the batting team. Henry Chadwick came up with the idea in 1858.

fair — in the playing area or territory between the foul lines, the white lines extending from home plate to the left-field and right-field foul poles.

fly, fly ball — a hit ball that rises high into the air. If it's caught before it touches the ground, the batter is out, a rule adopted by the New York Knickerbockers in 1865.

foul — in the area or territory outside the foul lines.

grand slam — a home run with the bases loaded. Borrowed from bridge (the card game), where it means one side captures all the cards, this term wasn't used in baseball until 1940.

ground ball — a batted ball that hits the ground in the infield and bounces or rolls; also called a **grounder**. When a player hits a grounder, he can **ground out** to an infielder.

hold the runner — keep a runner close to a base, usually by the pitcher throwing the ball (or pretending he might throw the ball) to the infielder in a **pickoff** move. The infielder must stay right at the bag.

inning — that part of a game during which each team has a chance to score until three of its players are out. Originally from the game of cricket, also used in horseshoes and bowling. The visiting team comes to bat in the **top of an inning**, the home team in the **bottom of an inning**. Spelled "innunge", and meaning "a getting in," the word existed before the year 900.

K — the symbol for strike-out. There are two explanations of its origin: (1) when Henry Chadwick made up a scoring system in 1861, he picked "K" as the most important letter in the word "strike" (he'd already used "S" for "sacrifice"); (2) when reporter and official scorer M.J. Kelly of the *New York Herald* made up a scoring system, he picked his own initial.

lineup — see **batting order**.

perfect game — a game in which no opposing player gets on base, that is, one team's pitcher gets all 27 of the other team's batters (3 outs x 9 innings) out in order. The most famous perfect game was pitched by Yankee Don Larson against the Brooklyn Dodgers in the 1956 World Series.

pick off — throw out a runner who has too big a "lead" off the base he was occupying. A pitcher is said to have a good **pickoff move**; a **pickoff play** happens when a pitcher or catcher throws suddenly to an infielder to catch a runner off base.

rookie — a player in his first full season as a pro. The word probably began as army slang for "recruit." English writer Rudyard Kipling used it in *Barrack-Room Ballads* in 1892.

sacrifice — a play in which the batter gives himself up — makes an out — in order to let a runner move up a base or come in to score. The batter either bunts or hits a fair or foul fly ball.

save — a credit that goes to a relief pitcher for protecting the lead for a starting pitcher. The save (S) became an official statistic in 1969.

shortstop — a position first known as "short fielder" and first played by Dr. Daniel Adams in 1849. His job was to relay the lightweight ball then in use from the outfield to the pitcher. Now the shortstop is part of the infield, playing just to the left of second base.

sign — a secret signal, using hands and fingers, either from catcher to pitcher for a particular kind of pitch; or from coach to batter or base runner for a particular play, such as bunt, hit-and-run, or steal.

spikes — small flattened knobs of metal, rubber or plastic on the sole and heel of a player's shoes, for better traction; the shoes themselves. To "spike" someone is to step on him, or slide into him feet first when wearing spikes.

strike zone — the space over home plate bounded by the sides of the plate, from a batter's armpits to his knees, when he is in his normal batting stance. Every umpire seems to have his own idea of the strike zone, despite the rule.

triple play — a play in which three putouts are made, one after the other. Former Oriole third baseman Brooks Robinson holds the record for hitting into triple plays — three.

walk — a base on balls. Four pitches out of the strike zone, at which a batter doesn't swing, earns him a walk to first base.

Index